SSL/TLS: UNDER LOCK AND KEY

❖

A Guide to Understanding SSL/TLS Cryptography

Paul Baka & Jeremy Schatten

SSL/TLS: UNDER LOCK AND KEY

Black and White Edition

by Paul Baka and Jeremy Schatten

Copyright © 2020 Keyko Pty Ltd. All rights reserved.

Keyko Pty Ltd

Suite 1A Level 2

802 Pacific Highway

Gordon NSW 2072

Australia

books@keyko.com.au

Edited by Sophie Pearce and Hollie Acres

Cover artwork by Ruslan Kholyaev

Formatting by Phillip Gessert

ISBN: 978-0-6489316-0-7 (*Colour Edition*)

ISBN: 978-0-6489316-3-8 (*Black and White Edition*)

ISBN: 978-0-6489316-2-1 (*PDF eBook*)

ISBN: 978-0-6489316-1-4 (*Reflowable eBook*)

ISBN: 978-0-6489316-4-5 (*Audiobook*)

All rights reserved. No part of this publication may be reproduced, distributed or transmitted in any form or by any means, including photocopying, recording, or other electronic or mechanical methods, without the prior written permission of the publisher, except in the case of brief quotations embodied in critical reviews and certain other noncommercial uses permitted by copyright law. For permission requests, write to the publisher at the address above.

The author and publisher have taken care in preparation of this book, but make no expressed or implied warranty of any kind and assume no responsibility for errors or omissions. No liability is assumed for incidental or consequential damages in connection with or arising out of the use of the information or programs contained herein.

TABLE OF Contents

INTRODUCTION: SCOPE AND AUDIENCE 1
    ABOUT THE AUTHORS 2
        PAUL BAKA 2
        JEREMY SCHATTEN 2
CHAPTER 1: SSL, TLS AND CRYPTOGRAPHY 3
    CRYPTOGRAPHY 3
        THE CAESAR CIPHER 4
    SYMMETRIC CRYPTOGRAPHY 5
    ASYMMETRIC CRYPTOGRAPHY 7
    SSL/TLS: THE BEST OF BOTH WORLDS 8
    HASHING 11
    DIGITAL SIGNATURES 12
    SSL VS. TLS: DEMYSTIFYING LEGACY TERMINOLOGY 12
    TRANSPORT LAYER SECURITY TLS 13
        TLS 1.0 13
        TLS 1.1 13
        TLS 1.2 14
        TLS 1.3 14

- KEY GENERATION 15
  - KEY SIZE 16
  - RSA 17
  - ECC 17
  - DES 17
  - AES 18

CHAPTER 2: COMMON PROTOCOLS 21

- HTTPS 21
  - HANDSHAKE PROTOCOL 22
  - KEY EXCHANGE 24
  - AUTHENTICATION 25
  - ENCRYPTION OVER HTTPS 28
  - RENEGOTIATION 29
  - CIPHER SUITES 29
  - CERTIFICATE TRANSPARENCY 30
  - SNI 31
  - HSTS 32
  - HPKP 33
  - PERFECT FORWARD SECRECY 33
- SMTPS 33
  - EXPLICIT SSL/TLS 34
  - STARTTLS 34
- FTPS 34
- LDAPS 35
- TCP 36

- DTLS (UDP) 36
- SCTP 37
- SPDY 37
- QUIC 37

CHAPTER 3: PUBLIC KEY INFRASTRUCTURE 39

CERTIFICATE LIFECYCLE 42
- KEY PAIR GENERATION 42
- CERTIFICATE SIGNING REQUEST 42
- VALIDATION 43
- ISSUANCE 43
- REVOCATION 43

CERTIFICATE AUTHORITIES 44
- ROOT CERTIFICATE AUTHORITIES 44
- INTERMEDIATE CERTIFICATE AUTHORITIES 45
- INTERNAL CERTIFICATE AUTHORITIES 46
- CERTIFICATE CROSS CERTIFICATION 46
- CRLS AND OCSP STAPLING 47
- CERTIFICATE AUTHORITY AUTHORISATION (CAA) 47
- MOST UTILIZED AND PUBLICLY TRUSTED CERTIFICATE AUTHORITIES 49

CHAPTER 4: X.509 CERTIFICATES 51

CERTIFICATE FIELDS 52
CERTIFICATE EXTENSIONS 54
TYPE OF CERTIFICATES 54
- STANDARD 54
- WILDCARD CERTIFICATES 55

- SAN/UCC CERTIFICATES ... 56
- CLIENT CERTIFICATES ... 57
- CODE SIGNING CERTIFICATES ... 57

CHAPTER 5: VULNERABILITIES AND FLAWS ... 59

- KEY SIZE ... 59
- MITM ATTACK ... 60
- UPSTREAM COMPROMISE ... 61
- KEY ESCROW ... 62
- PROXIES/MIDDLEBOXES ... 63
- DIGITAL SIGNATURE FORGERY ... 63
- SSL STRIPPING ... 64
- WELL-KNOWN ATTACKS ... 64
  - POODLE ... 65
  - HEARTBLEED ... 65
  - DROWN ... 66
  - CRIME, AND BREACH ... 66
  - TARGETED NATIONSTATE ATTACKS ... 67
  - QUANTUM COMPUTING ... 67

CHAPTER 6: IMPLEMENTATION ... 69

- A PLETHORA OF FILE FORMATS AND EXTENSIONS ... 69
  - BASE64 OR BINARY? ... 70
  - PUBLIC KEY, PRIVATE KEY, OR BOTH? ... 71
  - WINDOWS SCHANNEL ... 72
  - JAVA KEYSTORES ... 72
  - *NIX CONVENTIONS ... 72

  PKCS #7 AND PKCS #12 73

 PRIVATE KEY STORAGE 73

  HARDWARE SECURITY MODULE (HSM) 73

  DPAPI 73

  FILE SYSTEM ACLS 74

CHAPTER 7: OPENSSL 77

 SETUP AND USING OPENSSL 78

  WINDOWS 78

  MAC 78

  LINUX 78

 COMMON COMMANDS 79

  GENERATING A SELF SIGNED CERTIFICATE 79

  GENERATING A CSR FOR THIRD PARTY SIGNATURE 79

  CONVERTING A BINARY CERTIFICATE INTO A BASE64 CERTIFICATE 79

  CONVERTING A BASE64 CERTIFICATE INTO A BINARY CERTIFICATE 79

  SPLITTING A PKCS12 (PFX) INTO ITS COMPONENT PUBLIC AND PRIVATE KEYS 79

  COMBINING A BASE64 PUBLIC AND PRIVATE KEY INTO A PKCS12 (PFX) 79

  DISPLAY CERTIFICATES FROM A REMOTE SYSTEM 80

  GENERATING DIFFIE-HELLMAN PARAMETERS 80

  CHECKING KEY, FILE, AND CSR ASSOCIATION 80

CHAPTER 8: HTTP/2 AND HTTP/3 81

 EXCITING NEW FEATURES 82

 THE HTTPS EVERYWHERE MOVEMENT 83

CHAPTER 9: QUICK-START CONFIGURATION 85

 APACHE 85

- NGINX 91
- MICROSOFT WINDOWS AND IIS.. 97
  - SCHANNEL REGISTRY CHANGES 101
- JAVA AND TOMCAT 103
- CPANEL 104

TERMINOLOGY..111

INDEX 119

INTRODUCTION

Scope and Audience

SSL/TLS is an inherently complex topic; there are lots of resources and guides available that explain *how* to do something but very few which discuss *why*. This book seeks to address this gap, and in such a way that a beginner could pick this up, read through it cover to cover, and at least start to put together a mental map of the different facets of cryptography. SSL/TLS **must** be accessible to everyone because it is foundational to our modern online world. We need it to check our bank accounts, to talk to our friends online, and to compete in business. Though this book has been written for the beginner, meticulous attention has been paid to the layout such that an experienced professional could still find value in this writing as a desk reference. Finally, while it would be nice if this book serves a need, it is more important that it shares a passion. Each chapter has been written, and re-written with this in mind.

Feedback is greatly welcomed from our readers, and we will strive to keep it up-to-date and relevant. You may contact Paul via email books@keyko.com.au with any recommendations, ideas and general feedback.

About the Authors

Paul Baka

With over a decade of experience in web and online security, Paul has dedicated his career to ensuring that this sometimes complicated field is made accessible to those looking to secure their online privacy. With an intricate network of peers in the industry, Paul has not only built up his own knowledge and skill in this area, he has had the benefit of drawing knowledge from this network of field specialists. As an entrepreneur Paul has created multiple successful start-ups with a focus on the privacy of individuals and businesses alike.

When not dedicating himself to his work, Paul enjoys his time with family and friends, travelling and adventuring. With snow upon the mountains of Japan, Canada and Australia regularly carved by his well worn snowboard.

Jeremy Schatten

As a Systems Administrator with a background in Computer Science, Jeremy has never been able to pick between designing infrastructure and writing code. This inspired a lifelong fascination with digital cryptography as, like Jeremy, it has a foot in two worlds. Other than SSL/TLS, Jeremy's areas of technical expertise include Enterprise Storage, Virtualization, and software deployment pipelines. Unlike Paul, Jeremy is an avid indoorsman, and spends his non-screen time cooking, reading, and baking bread. He lives in Rockville, Maryland with his partner Kate and their cat Dorian Gray.

CHAPTER 1

SSL, TLS and Cryptography

Cryptography

Cryptography is the practice of creating and solving codes. It predates the earliest computers by over 1000 years! It can be used to hide important messages so that they can only be read by the intended recipient. In-fact, any attempt at obfuscating a message qualifies as a form of cryptography. One famous example of a cryptographic scheme is often performed by school children; milk (from the dairy aisle) is applied to a piece of paper with a Q-Tip in order to form letters, these letters are invisible unless the paper is given to someone in the know — by holding the paper up to the warmth of a light bulb, the sugars in the milk are gently burned, revealing the hidden message.

In the context of computer systems, "encryption" is a formalized cryptographic system making use of a different kind of hidden message - one that has been altered by applying a particular set of rules (or algorithm) known as a "cipher". Another set of rules can then be used to "decrypt" and change it back to its original form. The prototypical example of this is "3-back" or "The Caesar Cipher", famously regarded to have been the favorite way for Julius Caesar to communicate in secret.

The Caesar Cipher

The Caesar Cipher works by assigning each letter of the alphabet an ascending numerical value starting with A equal to 1, B equal to 2 and so on. We then replace each letter of our message with the letter whose numerical value is 3 less than the real letter, as displayed in the table below (Table 1.0).

A	=	X	H	=	E	O	=	L	V	=	S
B	=	Y	I	=	F	P	=	M	W	=	T
C	=	Z	J	=	G	Q	=	N	X	=	U
D	=	A	K	=	H	R	=	O	Y	=	V
E	=	B	L	=	I	S	=	P	Z	=	W
F	=	C	M	=	J	T	=	Q			
G	=	D	N	=	K	U	=	R			

Table 1.0: Caesar Cipher

I		L	O	V	E		C	R	Y	P	T	O	G	R	A	P	H	Y
F		I	L	S	B		Z	O	V	M	Q	L	D	O	X	M	E	V

Table 1.1: Caesar Cipher Example

Modern computers make use of an input to the cipher called a "key". The key is required to encrypt or decrypt the message. The two main subtypes of cryptography are differentiated by whether that key is the same for all parties involved (symmetric) or unique to each party (asymmetric).

Symmetric Cryptography

In Symmetric Cryptography, all parties share the same key to both encrypt and decrypt the message. Look again at the previous 3-back example, pretend that instead of 3-back, the cipher was "n-back" where n is a single digit number (0 - 9) known only to the parties privy to the communication. This would be a 4-bit key, since it takes 4 bits in binary to express the decimal range of 0 to 9.

While cryptographic systems vary in complexity, scale and design, cryptographers have agreed upon a set of standard terms. Some of these terms are:

- *"Plaintext" is the original message, unaltered.*
- *"Ciphertext" refers to the encoded message.*
- *"Encryption" is the act of converting plaintext into ciphertext, and*
- *"Decryption" is the act of converting a ciphertext back into plaintext by putting the cipher through its paces in reverse.*

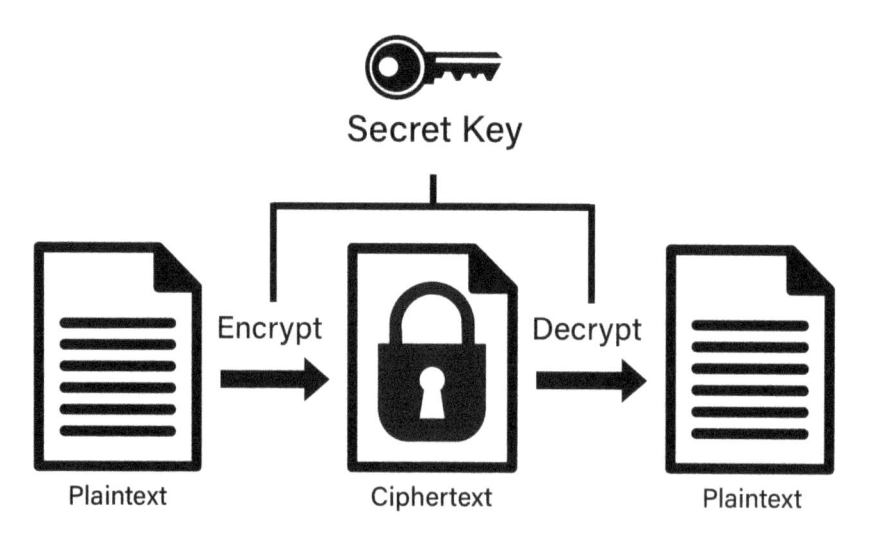

Image 1.0: Symmetric encryption

In digital practices, keys are much longer than 4 bits, and are derived from a key generation algorithm instead of being thought up. If a key, used to secure sensitive information, truly only had 10 possible values, that information would

Symmetric Cryptography is also commonly known as a "shared secret".

be very easy to guess! Although Symmetric Cryptography has some really great advantages, it also features some painful disadvantages.

Pros	It is extremely fast. Key management is very simple — there is only one key to manage.
Cons	As everyone shares the same key, it's impossible to figure out who's who in a conversation. At times, knowing who's who is really important, and being able to do it is referred to in cryptography as "non-repudiation".

Table 1.2: Symmetric Pros and Cons

This kind of cryptography requires the key to be transferred via a secure channel prior to the commencement of the communication. Otherwise, anyone eavesdropping on the wire will also have the private key and thus the ability to decrypt the private message. Not good!

Asymmetric Cryptography

In Asymmetric Cryptography, each participant has not one, but two keys. These keys are intrinsically linked. Information that is encrypted using the "public key", can then only be decrypted using the corresponding "private key".

The number of possible keys is referred to as the "keyspace". Ideally the keyspace should be large enough to deter anyone from attempting a Brute Force Attack, which is when every possible key is easily tested until the correct one is discovered.

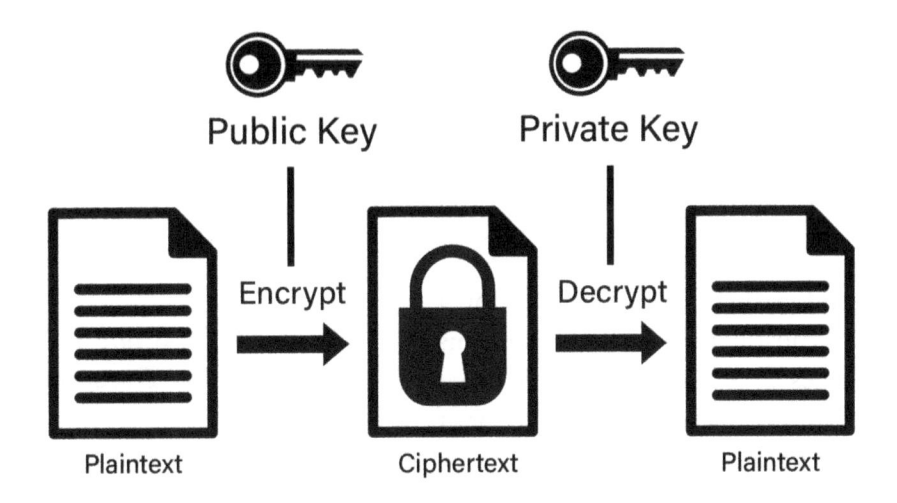

Image 1.1: Asymmetric encryption

The keys cannot be derived from each other without a prohibitively massive amount of computation. Mathematically, this relies on the factorization of large prime numbers and "one-way" functions which are easy to perform, but difficult to reverse. The opposite is also true; that which is encrypted using the private key can only be decrypted by the corresponding public key. In fact, this latter property is the foundation for digital signatures. Asymmetrical Cryptography comes with its own advantages and disadvantages.

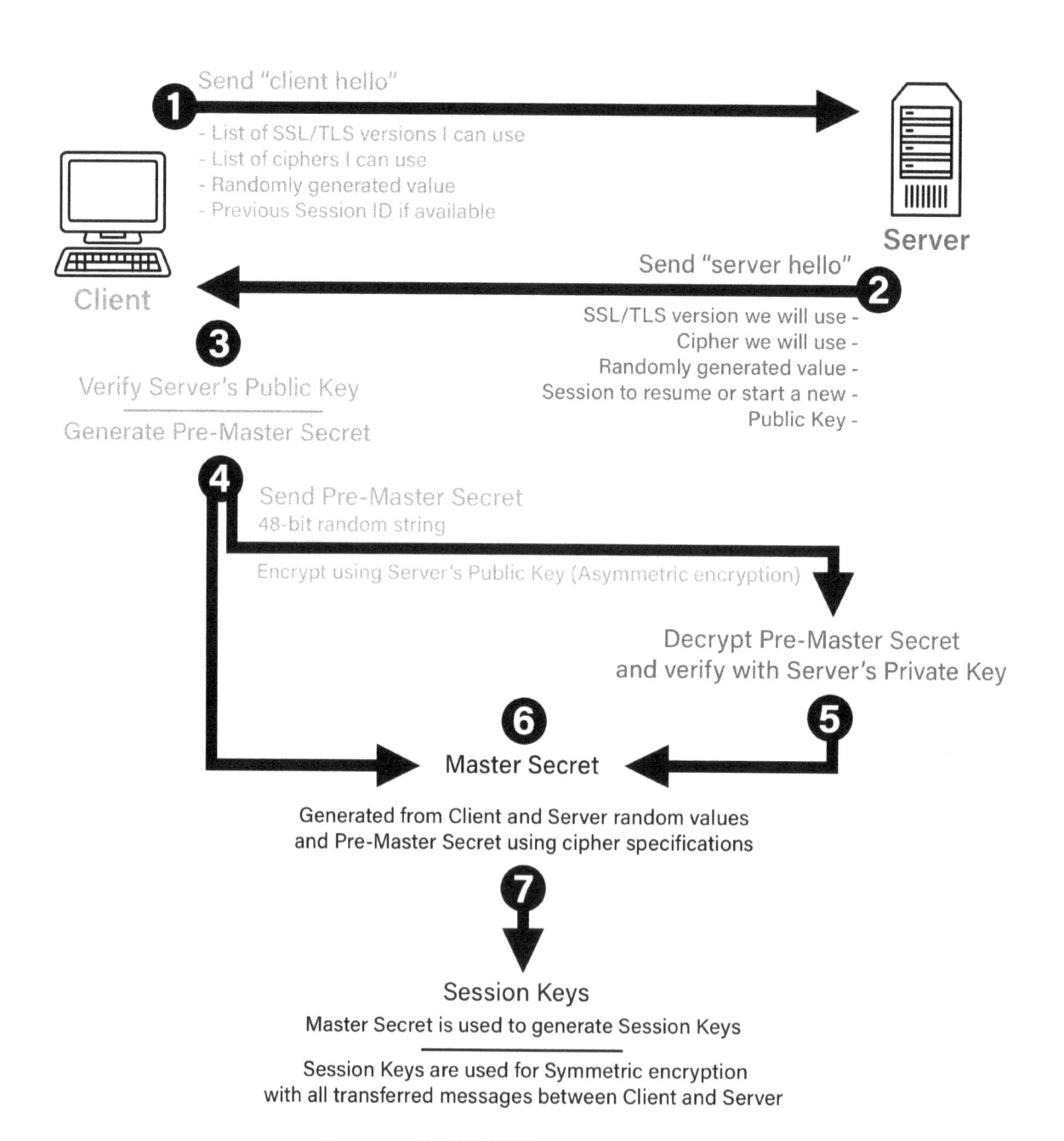

Image 1.2: The SSL/TLS handshake fundamentals

Hashing

A "hash" is simply the output of a one-way function: one that is easy to calculate, but too computationally expensive to reverse. This hash is guaranteed to be the same no matter how many times you run it through the hash generation algorithm. As this hash "describes" the original message, we sometimes also refer to a hash in this context as a "digest". Not all hash algorithms are built equally however.

As computers get more and more powerful, attackers are able to calculate "collisions" — that is, two different inputs which return the same hash output. Being able to create predictable collisions means that strategic padding of files can be used to make malicious content seem as if it were signed by someone else. For this reason, MD5 and SHA-1 are no longer considered suitable for cryptographic purposes. Try something like SHA-256 instead!

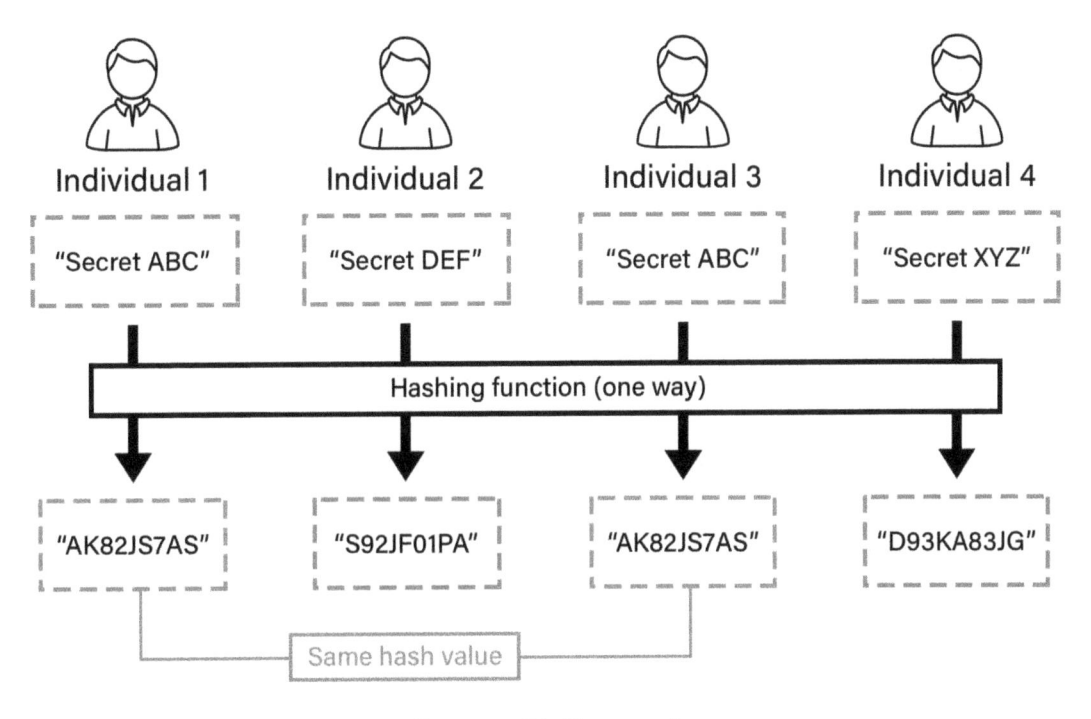

Image 1.3: Hashing example

Digital Signatures

Digital Signatures are a foundational concept in Cryptography. They are instrumental to the client's ability to validate the chain of trust as described previously. Digital Signatures take full advantage of the bidirectional relationship between public and private asymmetric keys.

Let's say you want to sign a block of text in such a way that the end recipient can verify that the text has arrived unaltered.

- First, you can run your text through an algorithm to generate a hash of the plaintext.
- Second, the hash is encrypted using the sender's asymmetric private key. This encrypted hash is delivered along with the message. In order to verify that the message was not altered in transit, the client first computes their own hash of the message using the same hash algorithm used by the sender.
- Lastly, the client decrypts the encrypted hash using the public asymmetric key, and matches it against the generated digest. If they match, this is an iron-clad guarantee that the integrity of the message is intact. Chapter 2: Encryption over HTTPS has more on this.

SSL vs. TLS: Demystifying legacy terminology

Before we dig deeper, it is worth unpacking the various ways in which SSL/TLS is described. SSL was the original protocol specification with Version 1; it was broken before it was fully introduced, and thus never supported. SSL 2 was deprecated in 2011, and SSL 3 officially put to bed in 2015. TLS is the direct successor of SSL. TLS 1.0 has been around since 1999, and been widely supported since the early 2000's. Many people will still refer to "TLS" as "SSL", and are merely being imprecise as opposed to differentiating between the two technologies. Others will refer only to TLS, which is correct, but isn't appropriate for all contexts, as oftentimes we discuss versions in relation to each other spanning protocol names. Referring to the topic as "SSL/TLS" is considered the most precise, unless followed by a version number such as "SSL 3.0" or "TLS 1.3".

Transport Layer Security TLS

TLS 1.0

TLS 1.0 was first defined by *RFC 2246*[2] in 1999. SSL 3.0 was rendered obsolete and was completely replaced by TLS 1.0. The standard for TLS 1.0 defines how connections are negotiated, what cipher options are available, and the degree of compatibility retained with SSL 3.0 and SSL 2.0.

TLS 1.0 supports both "stream ciphers" and "block ciphers" as did SSL 3.0. "Stream ciphers" encrypt data as it travels across the wire in real time. "Block ciphers" split the data up into segments of an agreed upon fixed size, encrypting those instead. Block ciphers are much more performant, and more frequently used. Part of encrypting each block of data is reliant on the result of the previous block. If implemented incorrectly, like dominoes, compromising one affects the integrity of the entire chain. TLS 1.0 does a poor job of mandating secure ciphers and is easy to configure with such weaknesses. Another pretty severe issue with TLS 1.0 is that if an error occurs (say due to a momentary network blip) the session cannot be resumed. Instead, the handshake must occur anew.

TLS 1.1

TLS 1.1, defined in *RFC 4246*[3], changed its initialization vector to be explicitly agreed upon (no longer relying on the previous block of data) in order to avoid the cipher block chaining (CBC) issue discussed above. This came at a steep performance cost, which at the time was considered enough of a reason for many businesses to stick with TLS 1.0 though at the cost of decreased security. Today, with modern hardware, the difference is negligible. TLS 1.1 also allowed sessions to resume, even if the connection was terminated without either party initiating the end of communication. TLS 1.1 was considered to be a secure protocol revision well into the prominence of TLS 1.2. Even so, it is infrequently used in the wild, as TLS 1.1 and 1.2 came out so close together.

---

2. *https://www.rfc-editor.org/info/rfc2246*
3. *https://www.rfc-editor.org/info/rfc4246*

TLS 1.2

TLS 1.2, defined in *RFC 5246*[4], has relatively few features beyond TLS 1.1. It can be argued that it is mostly a formalization of best practices. A handful of decisions that were previously left up to the software designers were mandated for consistency's sake.

TLS_RSA_WITH_AES_128_CBC_SHA became a cipher that was required to be supported for all software implementing TLS 1.2. This helped define the best cipher to use when testing web server performance. Finally, support was included for SHA-2 digital signatures and message authentication. At the time of this writing, SHA-1 has only recently been considered a serious security risk.

TLS 1.3

TLS 1.3 was defined in *RFC 8446*[5], and has some massive performance implications. Historically, establishing a secure channel from client to server required 3 round trips to be made. First, the TCP channel needed to perform its 3-way handshake. Next, TLS required two 2 round trips before data could be sent across the secure channel. For clients that support it, *RFC 7413*[6] defines a standard for "TCP Fast Open". This allows the client to send additional data along with its first request. This "primes the pump", and allows the server to begin formulating a response before it has even finished its handshake with the client. This does not compromise the integrity of the SSL/TLS handshake, as the initial request is sent in the clear anyway. This saves us an entire round trip.

RFC 7918[7] defines an improvement in TLS 1.3 for supported clients called "TLS False Start". Similar to TCP Fast Open, this allows data to be sent along with the SSL/TLS handshake so the server can get started preparing a response. If the handshake never goes through, the server can simply discard its prepared reply. Finally, TLS 1.3 introduces 0-round trip resumption (0-RTT) that allows a client who has communicated recently with the server to start sending encrypted data without renegotiating the handshake at all. Unfortunately, if an attacker were to replay this traffic at just the right time, the server wouldn't be able to tell the difference between legitimate traffic and the replayed traffic. This

---

4. https://www.rfc-editor.org/info/rfc5246
5. https://www.rfc-editor.org/info/rfc8446
6. https://www.rfc-editor.org/info/rfc7413
7. https://www.rfc-editor.org/info/rfc7918

makes 0-RTT an excellent choice for a read-only API, but a poor choice for an application that blindly accepts an HTTP POST or PUT.

Not only does TLS 1.3 increase performance, but it also enhances security. TLS 1.3 effectively mandates Perfect Forward Secrecy (Chapter 2: PFS). By using an algorithm known as Diffie-Hellman, the symmetric key used to encrypt data is constantly rotating throughout the communication. If PFS is not used, the compromise of a server's private key means an attacker could decrypt everything encrypted since the server started using that key. In previous versions of TLS, PFS was dependent upon the cipher negotiated between the server and the client. TLS 1.3 on the other hand, consciously only supports ciphers which conform to this PFS property.

TLS 1.3 removes support for many weaker cipher suites (such as RC4) which are unfortunately still very common on the internet at large.

Key Generation

In SSL/TLS, Key Generation refers to the act of creating a key that will be used to encrypt or decrypt data. A particular strategy for generating a key that can be used in this manner is referred to as a "key generation algorithm"[8]. Key generation algorithms can be either symmetric or asymmetric. Symmetric key generation algorithms produce a single key, used by all parties. Asymmetric key generation is more complicated; it outputs two intrinsically linked keys — the public and private keys discussed above.

---

8. An algorithm is best defined as a series of steps that guarantees a particular result

Key Size

Key size refers to the length of the key material (in bits). The "key space" refers to every possible combination of bits of that length. Iterating through every possible combination is referred to as a "brute force attack" (Chapter 5: Key Size) — you can think of it as buying up every lottery ticket to guarantee that you win. Whether a given key size is considered secure or not depends on how long it would take an attacker to "guess and check" each attempt. For example, a 2048 bit RSA key is considered to be secure because it would take more time to try every possible combination with today's computers, than time that our universe has existed. For Elliptic Curve based cryptography, a 256 bit key provides a roughly similar safety net.

Table 1.4 outlines current (2018) recommended minimum key sizes for various encryption methods, and their expected service life. As technology improves and speeds increase, the encryption also needs to become more complex through increasing the key size.

Protection	Symmetric	RSA / DSA / DH	Elliptic curve crypto	Hash
Legacy standard level *Should not be used in new systems*	80	1024	160	160
Near term protection *Security for at least ten years (2020-2028)*	128	3072	256	256
Long-term protection *Security for thirty to fifty years (2020-2068)*	256	15360	512	512

Table 1.4
Source: Encryption strength for commonly used key sizes. ECRYPT-CSA Recommendations (2018)

RSA

RSA was named after its creators Ron Rivest, Adi Shamir, and Leonard Adleman, in 1977. RSA is one of the most commonly used asymmetric key generation algorithms. It relies on the factorization of two randomly generated large prime numbers to come up with a related public and private key. If these prime numbers were known to an attacker, they would be able to easily generate the private key based upon the public key. Without these inputs however; the relationship between the public and private key is not immediately apparent. Only by brute forcing all possible keys (guess and check) can this relationship be reversed. These large prime numbers are discarded after the keys are generated – they are not needed again. At the time of this writing, RSA keys of 2048 bits or greater are considered to be of a sufficient length that makes brute forcing the keyspace impractical.

Then why don't we use massive keys in order to be future-proof? Unfortunately, the larger the key, the longer it takes to encrypt or decrypt data. Asymmetric encryption is slow, and that is why RSA is used in SSL/TLS in order to encrypt a symmetric key that can then be used to encrypt and decrypt data much faster.

ECC

ECC (Elliptic Curve Cryptography); instead of relying on large prime numbers, ECC relies on the mathematical properties of parabolic curves. Similarly to RSA, a mathematically linked public and private key are generated. However; the key size for the same level of security can be much smaller using ECC, since brute forcing the keyspace is much more computationally intensive. For example; With ECC, a 224-bit ECC key is as difficult to break as a 2048-bit RSA key. ECC is also considered to be less likely to be broken by the advent of quantum computers, which have proven to be very good at quickly attempting to reverse the factorization of large prime numbers.

DES

In the 1970s, the United States National Bureau of Standards (NBS) put out a request for proposals; they were seeking an algorithm that met certain properties in order to standardize a symmetric key algorithm for government use. IBM submitted the most compelling algorithm, which was formalized as the Data Encryption Standard (DES).

DES is a block cipher; it operates on 64 bits of data at a time, using 56-bit keys and 6 bits of arbitrary padding. DES mixes the plaintext message with the key in such a way that the only way to decrypt it is to have access to the symmetric key. DES has three main "modes":

1. Electronic Code Book (ECB),
2. Chain Block Coding (CBC), and
3. Cipher Feedback (CFB).

In ECB mode, each block of 64 bits is simply encrypted individually with the 56-bit key. In CBC and CFB mode, each subsequent block relies (like dominoes) on the output of some of the preceding blocks.

In 1997, the NIST announced that they required a replacement for DES, whose keysize had rendered the algorithm susceptible to being brute forced by computers of that time. In fact, in 1998 the Electronic Frontier Foundation (EFF) created a purpose-built DES cracking machine. A variant of DES, 3DES was created to extend the lifetime of the DES algorithm. By performing staggered DES operations with three different keys, the ciphertext becomes much more computationally expensive to crack.

AES

In 2001, the Rijndael Block Cipher was chosen as direct successor to DES. It is considered to be the new Advanced Encryption Standard (AES). AES uses key sizes of 128, 192, or 256 bits. It is commonly used in SSL/TLS today in order to perform symmetric encryption. In addition to being more secure, AES is also much faster than 3DES.

Like DES, AES:

- Is a block cipher,
- Operates on 128 bits of data at a time, regardless of keysize
- Has an ECB, a CBC and a CFB mode.

However; AES also has 2 additional modes; Output Feedback (OFB), and Counter (CTR) mode.

In OFB mode, AES acts on a continuous stream of data like a stream cipher, even though it is a block cipher. This ability makes AES in OFB mode extremely flexible.

CTR mode, like OFB mode, allows AES to operate on a stream of data, however CTR mode also introduces optimisations that allow the encryption to be "divided and conquered" across multiple threads. DES could only operate in a single-threaded capacity so AES's ability to play nicely with parallel programming is a huge bonus.

CHAPTER 2

Common Protocols

SSL/TLS is protocol agnostic, meaning; in theory, any protocol can be tunnelled through it. This chapter however, looks at the most commonly seen protocols used over SSL/TLS 'in the wild'. With the focus on HTTPS, other protocols will be discussed only in relation to how they differ in practice from the implementation of HTTP over SSL/TLS.

HTTPS

Overview

HTTP (Hyper-Text Transfer Protocol) is a Layer 7 protocol[1], first defined in *RFC 1945*[2]. It is used as the protocol for transferring enriched text (hyper-text) over a network. Enriched text is simply text that contains metadata along with the text. This metadata can be; a link, an image, or a formatting instruction.

---

1. Layer 7 refers to the "Application Layer" of the OSI model, which is a common way of describing how computers communicate over a network. Application Layer protocols must communicate over a Transport Layer (Layer 4) protocol, in this case, TCP
2. *https://www.rfc-editor.org/info/rfc1945*

An application living on a server somewhere will bind to a "socket" (a specific IP address and port) on its Operating System and will listen for incoming connections. If this application is a web server that speaks HTTP, it is likely to respond with a mix of HTML, CSS, and Javascript which will then be rendered by the client browser on the other end of the connection. The client and server at this point have already negotiated over TCP. You can think of TCP like a train tunnel and HTTP like a train. To further this analogy, SSL/TLS would be the shade of tinting applied to the windows of the train.

Handshake Protocol

In a HTTPS session, the first handshake that is performed is the TCP handshake. TCP is a Layer 4 protocol[3].

TCP utilizes a three-way handshake in order to establish a connection. First, the client announces its intention to begin a conversation by sending a message known as a "SYN". The server responds with "SYN-ACK", a message including a hint as to what sequence number it will use when the communication begins in earnest. Finally, the client sends an "ACK" to let the server know that it's ready to begin the conversation.

The second handshake in an HTTPS session is the SSL/TLS handshake. The HTTPS client (your web browser) and the HTTPS server need to agree on what protocol version to use, what ciphers to employ and whether or not to mutually authenticate. Usually, mutual authentication is not required, and the only authentication that must occur is for the client to chain the server's public key to a known Root Certificate Authority. From here, the asymmetric portion of SSL/TLS occurs, and a symmetric key is decided upon via this secure channel. That agreed upon key will be used to communicate going forward over the protocol of choice — HTTP.

---

3. A Layer 4 (Transport Layer) protocol handles things such as retransmission of dropped segments, ordering of the packets inside the segments and error checking.

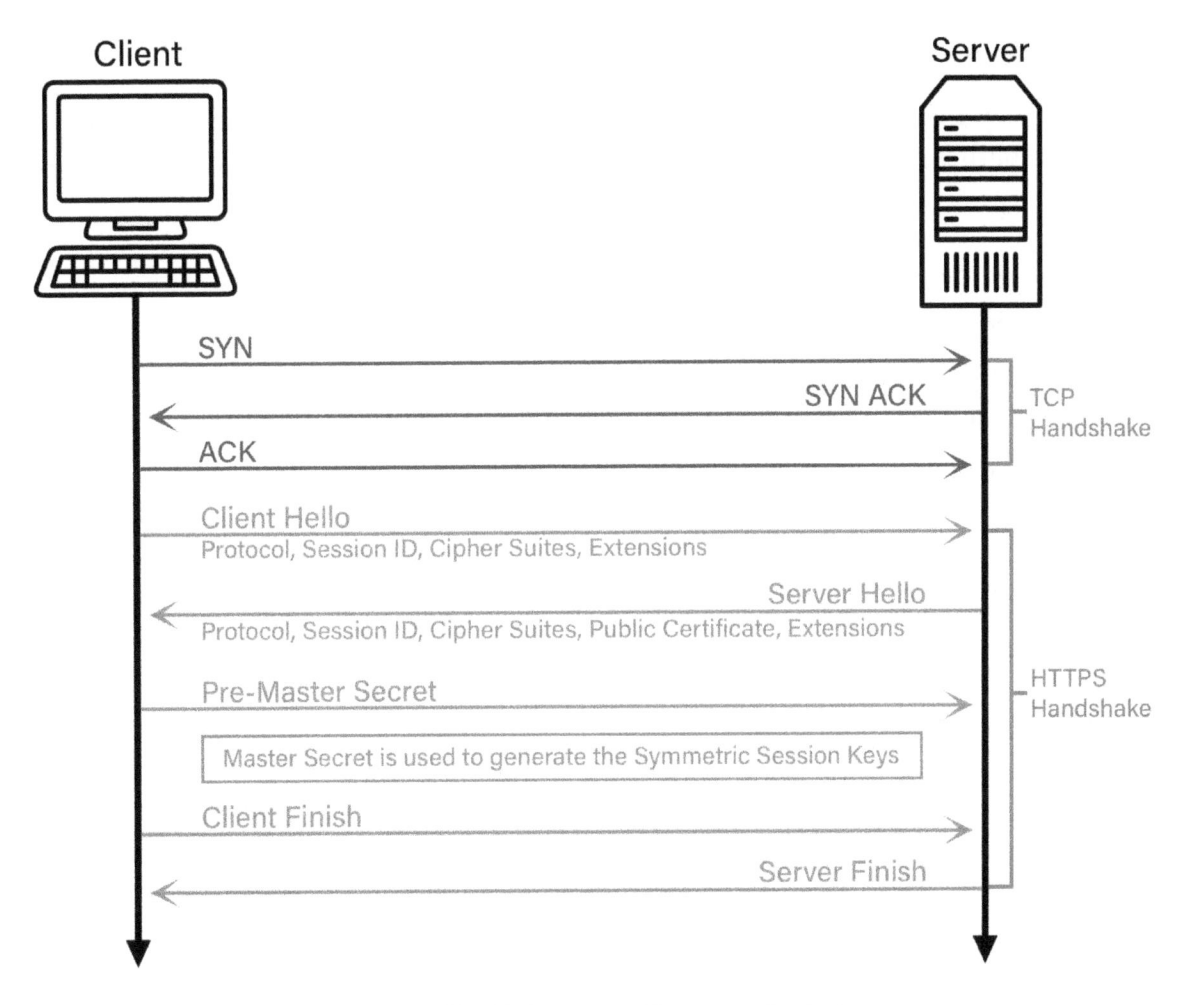

Image 2.0: Handshake process with server authentication

Key Exchange

How does Key Exchange occur during the SSL/TLS handshake? With the TCP channel already established, the client sends a "client hello" to the server. Included in this message is:

- A list of the protocol versions the client supports (ordered in preference from left to right)
- A 32-bit random number (this number will later be mixed with the server's random number in order to generate the symmetric key)
- A session ID
- Supported compression methods
- Supported cipher suites
- Any known extensions to the SSL/TLS protocol that it wishes to request.

Next, the server sends a "server hello" containing; the protocols, cipher suites, compression methods, and extensions it supports, as well as a randomly generated 32-bit number. The server also sends its public key. At this point, the client will attempt to verify trust with the server's public key. This involves finding a valid path that will chain a root certificate which the client already explicitly trusts, to the server's public key, potentially traversing other intermediate certificate authorities in the process. If the client trusts the server (and mutual authentication is not required), the client will compute what's known as the "pre-master" secret and encrypt it using the server's public key before sending it to the server. The server decrypts this value using its private key. Both the client and the server compute the "master secret" independently, arriving at the same result because they are working with the same inputs! This master secret is used to generate session keys (symmetric key) used for the duration of the session. How that encryption occurs is dependent upon the negotiated cipher suite.

Authentication

Usually when we use HTTPS we are only performing one-way authentication. The end user client needs to authenticate the server. If a user needs to login, it will be performed by the application, not by SSL/TLS. However, if the client does not authenticate the server, an attacker listening on the wire is able to perform all manner of mischief.

For example; an attacker hiding on the same Layer 2[4] adjacent network as the client has the ability to proxy or redirect traffic to anywhere they please by sending fake broadcast frames (known as ARP poisoning). Even though the data may be encrypted through transit, it's heading straight to the imposter who decrypts it! Therefore, it is equally important to ensure that not only are we sending data in a way that's safe from nosy people, but that we know that we are sending data to the party we intend.

But how exactly does an end user client determine whether to trust a particular server? Within the handshake process, the server responds in the "server hello" with its public certificate. This public certificate contains the server's public key and a digital signature from a trusted third party. This trusted third party is known as the Certificate Authority. The Certificate Authority had taken a digest of the certificate using a hashing algorithm. Then, it uses this hash to generate the signature appended to the certificate. The end user client also computes their own hash of the server's public certificate. The client uses this generated hash and the Certificate Authority's public key (which has been pre-installed on the client's computer/device), to verify the certificate signature through cipher algorithms.

---

[4]. In layer 2 of the OSI model, Ethernet "frames" are broadcast to the entire local subnet. Computers listen for traffic intended for them, and ignore other frames. Imagine bringing in the mail for your flatmates and handing it out. There's inherently a certain amount of trust involved, especially if someone's grandma sends them birthday money!

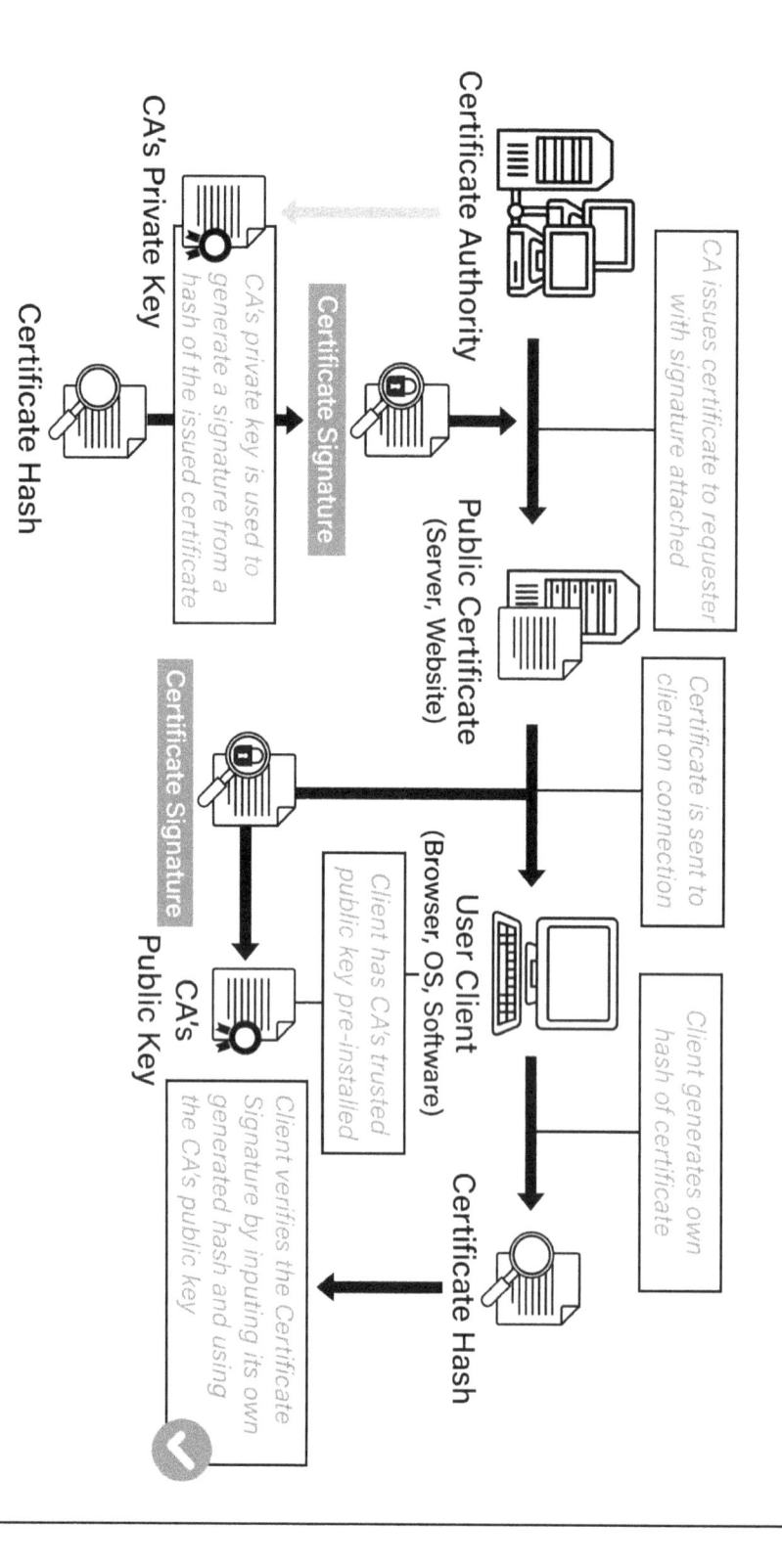

Image 2.1: Validation of Certificate via Signature

26 • HTTPS

Sometimes, there is more than one Certificate Authority between the server's certificate signature and the "Root Certificate Authority" which the client's browser is pre-installed with. In this case, the client has an extra step it needs to do: repeat this process on any Intermediate Certificate Authority's public key which the server serves along with its own public key or any intermediate certificate the client is already aware of. (Some browsers come pre-installed with intermediate certificate authorities as well.). Any valid path, from a Root CA the client already trusts to the certificate the client is attempting to verify, results in trusting the server. The lack of such a valid path will cause the client to report an error and terminate the connection.

Some organizations do elect to use mutual authentication as a means of multi-factor authentication in order to uniquely identify a device. The device will be provisioned with a unique SSL/TLS certificate as part of a private PKI (Public Key Infrastructure, see Chapter 3), and a reverse proxy will be employed using certificate authentication (mutual authentication).

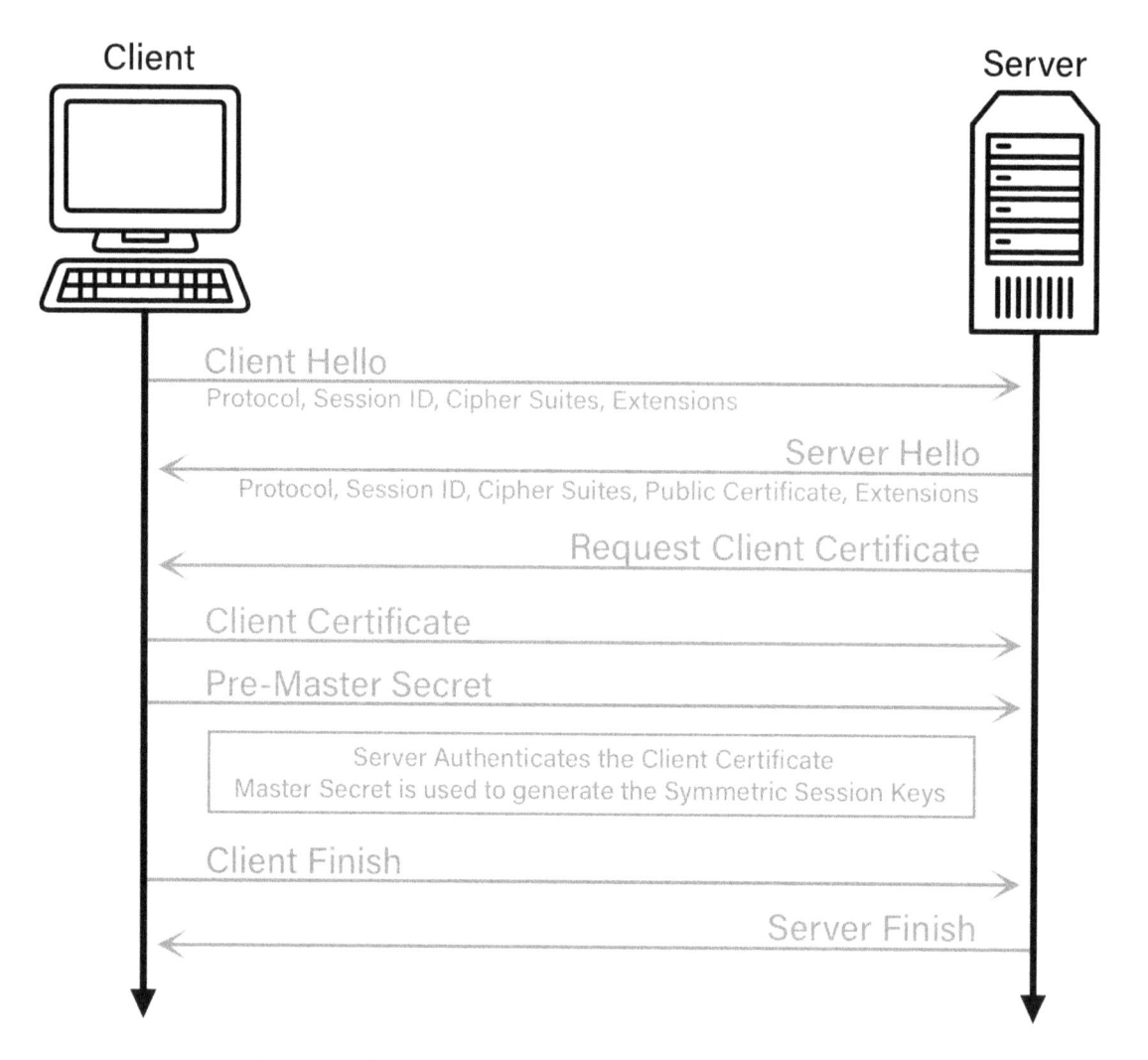

Image 2.2: Handshake process with server and client authentication

Encryption over HTTPS

The handshake, as described previously, happens in the open. Asymmetric encryption is used to establish the initial channel, over which only the symmetric key is sent. Once both sides have agreed upon the symmetric key, all further communication is encrypted using this key. The algorithm used to encrypt is determined by the agreed upon cipher. Without knowing this symmetric key, an attacker listening on the wire will not be able to make sense of what appears to be only random data.

Renegotiation

SSL/TLS provides a mechanism for either the client or the server to "change their mind" and request the usage of a different cipher suite or protocol version. This can be requested by either the client or the server. Unfortunately, over the years, there have been a number of vulnerabilities linked to not properly validating which SSL/TLS session was renegotiating. Attempts to fix this were included as SSL/TLS extensions later on. To avoid confusion, the original specification is referred to as "insecure renegotiation" and the version taking advantage of the extension is referred to as "secure renegotiation".

Cipher Suites

A "Cipher Suite" refers to a combination of options, working together, that act as inputs to SSL/TLS in order to define how to communicate securely.

For example, the following cipher suite is one of the 5 supported by TLS 1.3.

TLS_AES_128_GCM_SHA256

TLS	The TLS protocol (as opposed to SSL).
AES	The algorithm used for the symmetric portion of the encryption.
128	The key size used by AES. (AES is capable of using 3 different key sizes, 128, 192, and 256 bits)
GCM	Refers to AES being used in "Counter Mode" one of the different ways AES can encrypt and decrypt a key. "Counter Mode" allows AES, a block cipher, to act like a stream cipher, and lends itself well to be split up amongst multiple threads on multiple cores via multiprogramming.
SHA256	The hashing algorithm used to compute digital signatures.

Table 2.0: TLS_AES_128_GCM_SHA256 Cipher

TLS 1.3 changes how cipher suites are formatted to specify only the symmetric cryptography options. (The asymmetric portion in TLS 1.3 is now static, so no options need be specified).

In TLS 1.2 and below, a cipher might have looked like this:

TLS_DHE_RSA_WITH_AES_128_GCM_SHA256

TLS	Once again, refers to the protocol.
DHE	Refers to "Diffie Hellman Ephemeral", a key exchange algorithm.
RSA	The asymmetric encryption algorithm used.
AES	Refers to the symmetric encryption algorithm used.
GCM	Like in TLS 1.3, denotes AES runs in counter mode.
SHA256	Refers to the hashing algorithm, the same as in the newer cipher suites.

Table 2.1: TLS_DHE_RSA_WITH_AES_128_GCM_SHA256 Cipher

Certificate Transparency

Certificate Transparency (defined in *RFC 6962*[5]) defines a standardized format for exposing public logs of issued certificates and thereby protecting users. It has three main goals:

1. Make visible to a domain owner any certificate issued by a certificate authority.
2. Have a publicly available auditing and monitoring system, allowing CAs and domain owners to determine whether certificates have been mistakenly or maliciously issued.
3. Protect users from mistakenly or maliciously issued certificates.

The goals are addressed through the three components of an open framework for monitoring and auditing certificates:

Certificate Logs

These logs are essentially databases that maintain a list of certificates. They may be maintained independently by a CA, ISP or any other interested parties. Anyone can query a log

---

5. *https://www.rfc-editor.org/info/rfc6962*

to verify that a particular certificate has been logged. When a certificate is issued, it should be added to a log.

Monitors

These are publicly run servers that query all log servers and watch for suspicious certificates, such as a certificate that has been illegitimately issued for a domain.

These monitoring servers may be run by interested parties such as internet companies like Google, or banks and governments. Anyone has the ability to run their own monitoring service or subscribe to monitoring services offered.

Auditors

These are software components that typically verify that logs are correct and consistent, and also verify that a particular certificate appears in a log. If a certificate does not appear in a log, it will be treated as a suspicious certificate and it may not be trusted.

An inbuilt auditing service can be an integral part of a browser to help protect the user.

SNI

"Server Name Indication" (SNI) refers to an extension (Chapter 4: Certificate Extensions) of the SSL/TLS protocol.

When using TLS, a secure session needs to be created before any host header[6] information is available to the server. If the server is hosting only one website, it is clear which certificate and private key to use as there is only the one. The problem is; for any server that is hosting multiple websites, with host header information not yet available at this stage, it becomes unclear which site to serve alongside which certificate, in order to establish the secure connection.

In 2018, Google Chrome made a policy decision to only include root certificates from CAs which provide public logs. Due to this, and other industry pressures, Certificate Transparency is available (almost) across the board.

This is where SNI comes in; when the client is establishing the connection to the web server and doing the TLS handshake, it will include the hostname (domain name) of the

---

6. The Host Header identifies the server/domain requested by the client.

requested website/service. The web server will now know which certificate and private key to use to establish the secure connection.

Today, all modern browsers support the SNI extension, but there is also a server side mechanism for specifying what to do when a connecting client doesn't support SNI. (Many sites will redirect to an error page with their browser requirements. Some might pick a default site to direct traffic for older clients. Others still might issue a redirect to another hostname on another port).

HSTS

HTTP Strict Transport Security (HSTS) (defined in *RFC 6797*[7]) provides a way for a Server Administrator to assert a set of additional rules that a client should follow in relation to their site. HSTS is a promise from a server that it only makes itself available over HTTPS now and in the future. Browsers maintain a cache, and will refuse to connect over HTTP to that domain. this protects against SSL Stripping attacks (Chapter 5: SSL Stripping). However, this means that to be protected from an attack, a user will have had to visit that specific site at least once to prime the cache. This is where the HSTS "preload" directive comes in. If the server administrator configures this directive, the site becomes available for browser providers to include it in their list of HSTS sites deployed on browser install. It removes the requirement that a user must visit the site to enjoy protection — HTTPS Stripping attacks will be thwarted from the very first site visit. HSTS also provides a mechanism for server administrators to include all subdomains.

---

7. *https://www.rfc-editor.org/info/rfc6797*

HPKP

HTTP Public Key Pinning (HPKP) is living proof that sometimes things fail despite the best of intentions. Rarely used successfully, support for HPKP has been removed in many browsers completely due to rampant misconfiguration. HPKP provided a mechanism for Administrators to announce their intention. For example; HPKP could be used for providing a trusted hash of the root certificate, or server certificate, required to be accepted for visiting a website. Along with this hash comes the maximum age, directly corresponding to the expiration date of the certificate. Unfortunately, once the site proved untrustworthy (perhaps when changing to a certificate signed by a different CA) there was no way to recant, and it was too easy for Administrators to "lock their keys in the car".

Perfect Forward Secrecy

Perfect Forward Secrecy (PFS) refers to a property of an encryption scheme which ensures that the compromise of the private key sometime in the future does not allow past traffic to be decrypted. This is accomplished via an algorithm called Diffie-Hellman, which rotates the symmetric portion of the key constantly during the session. Without this property, an attacker could passively sniff traffic and sit on it for decades, hoping security standards change and a powerful enough computer will come along that can brute force the key. PFS is a facet of the choice for a negotiated cipher.

Up to TLS 1.2, only some ciphers supported PFS (check to see if they include DHE or ECDHE in their name), but as of TLS 1.3, only ciphers that support PFS are supported by the protocol.

SMTPS

The Simple Mail Transfer Protocol (SMTP) is widely used for sending and receiving email. Unfortunately, due to its age, this protocol was not designed with security in mind. Bolted on after the fact, SMTPS is simply plaintext SMTP sent over an SSL/TLS channel. The implementation of SMTPS is a little more complex than other protocol's. Due to this complexity two opposing implementations have become popular; Explicit SSL/TLS, and Start-TLS.

Explicit SSL/TLS

Plaintext SMTP usually occurs over port 25. SMTPS however, typically occurs over ports 465 or 587. Why two ports? Port 465 was selected randomly by the IANA[8] and never standardized in any sort of RFC. It was intended for SMTP over SSL. Very shortly thereafter, TLS came onto the scene, and port 587 was properly codified for SMTP over TLS. You will often see Explicit SSL/TLS used by SMTP on Linux or Unix systems.

StartTLS

StartTLS allows for an already established plaintext session to "upgrade" itself to a secure session. Either the client or the server may request this upgrade. After exchanging information during the SMTP handshake, most clients will request encryption. This method of upgrading an already in-play session is referred to as "opportunistic TLS". The original plaintext session establishes a connection over port 25, and even when the conversation is upgraded to be encrypted, it remains over port 25. Thus knowing what port the communication occurs over is not enough to determine whether or not the connection is or was encrypted!

FTPS

FTPS is simply File Transfer Protocol (FTP) over SSL/TLS. It is used to transmit files across the wire, either in binary or ASCII mode. FTP defines both an active and a passive mode.

- **Active mode**: the server initiates the data transfer *after* the client has connected to the server.
- **Passive mode**: the client initiates the data transfer.

These opposing modes can make configuring support for FTP or FTPS within your firewall very complicated. A lot of firewalls are coded to inspect the initial conversation and

---

8. IANA; The Internet Assigned Numbers Authority maintain a list assigning services to default ports

open up ports on-the-fly, but if encrypted, this is not possible. Therefore, FTPS is better suited for active mode, as it will occur over a single port.

FTPS should not be confused with SFTP, which is part of the SSH protocol. Although it is also used to transfer files securely, SSH does not use SSL/TLS at all, and instead it establishes a secure connection using similar cryptographic techniques.

LDAPS

The Lightweight Directory Access Protocol (LDAP) is defined in *RFC 4511*[9]. It provides a means of publishing directory listings as well as a query language, used to retrieve information from the system. Microsoft's implementation of LDAP is called "Active Directory" (AD) and is the de facto backbone for authentication within the Enterprise.

OpenLDAP is often used in non-Microsoft Windows environments. LDAPS is simply LDAP over SSL/TLS. Like SMTP, LDAP can leverage either explicit SSL/TLS or Start-TLS. LDAP (and LDAP with StartTLS) occur over port 389, LDAPS defaults to port 636.

Most information in an LDAP system is public by default — usernames, first names, last names, email addresses, and even "favorite beverage" are all "attributes" LDAP is primed to store. The notable exception to this are password hashes, which should not be returned, but rather compared, for LDAP to make an authentication decision.

---

9. *https://www.rfc-editor.org/info/rfc4511*

TCP

While relatively uncommon, SSL/TLS can be used directly over a TCP (Transmission Control Protocol) connection. Typically, a layer 7 protocol like HTTP would run over TCP and that would be wrapped in SSL/TLS. However; sometimes developers, for performance reasons, prefer to communicate simple messages directly to a program listening on a TCP socket. TCP is the transport protocol of choice for the vast majority of communication on the internet. Via its three way handshake, it provides confirmation that each segment has been transmitted, as well as a mechanism for correctly reordering segments that have arrived out of order, and for requesting retransmission of a segment lost in transit.

DTLS (UDP)

UDP (User Data Protocol), unlike TCP, does not provide receipt confirmation, UDP segments are fired and forgotten. This method utilises less overhead, and in certain situations is extremely useful. For example, streaming video, which has a high tolerance for errors. A few lost segments might not even be noticed by the end user, and even many lost segments might result in the loss of only a single frame of video. SSL/TLS however, requires a reliable transport stream like TCP. This is where Datagram Transport Layer Security (DTLS) comes into play. Technically speaking, it is an entirely different protocol from SSL/TLS, but still worth touching on briefly in this book. DTLS is defined in *RFC 6347*[10]. DTLS is interesting, because it provides the reliable transport features it needs over an inherently unreliable transport, but only for the duration of establishing a symmetric key. DTLS is rarely used in practice, but is an option for encrypting UDP traffic across the wire.

---

10. *https://www.rfc-editor.org/info/rfc6347*

SCTP

SCTP, like TCP or UDP, is a transport layer (layer 4) protocol. It is fair to say that most administrators have not worked with it directly, but it is the transport protocol of choice for LTE cellular networks. It uses many parallel streams to achieve high transfer rates, and is an excellent choice when the physical layer is different for transmit than receive (backhaul). Like UDP, DTLS can be implemented on top of SCTP.

SPDY

SPDY, now deprecated, is important to discuss because it served as a proof-of-concept for HTTP/2, and added a session layer on top of SSL/TLS in order to reduce traffic going back and forth. SPDY leveraged TCP, and this experiment wound up exposing a lot of inefficiencies inherent to TCP as a transport mechanism. QUIC later went on to build its own sessioning atop UDP for even starker performance gains.

QUIC

QUIC takes a lot of inspiration from SCTP, and provides its own sessioning on top of UDP. HTTP over QUIC is the basis for the IETF's HTTP/3 protocol which is a big deal, because for the very first time SSL/TLS is a first class citizen. In HTTP/3, there is no such thing as an unencrypted connection.

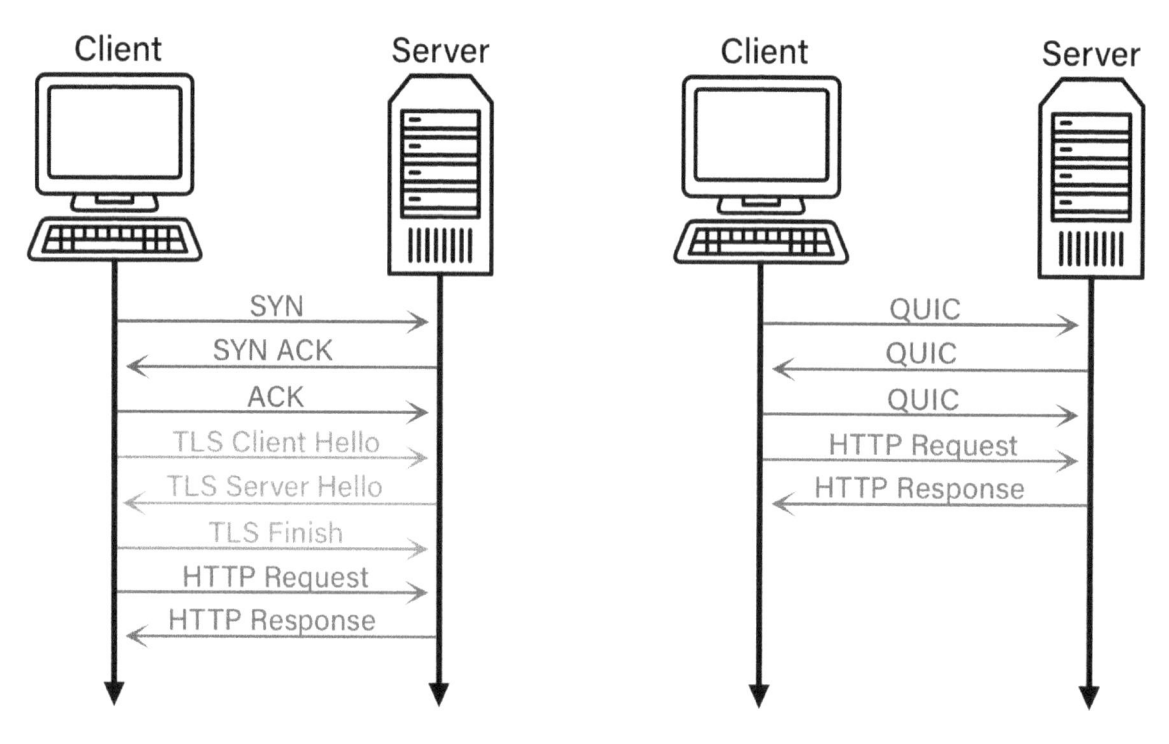

Image 2.3: HTTP Request Over TCP + TLS vs Over QUIC

CHAPTER 3

Public Key Infrastructure

While SSL/TLS defines a way to exchange secure information over an insecure channel, "Public Key Infrastructure" (PKI) refers to a formalised system for employing encryption to perform a task. How is this utilised in the real world?

SSL/TLS makes two different promises, and thus far, we have only explored the first promise: encryption. Encryption deals with data being sent in such a way that an attacker listening on the wire can't make heads or tails of it. The second promise, authentication, is achieved through a PKI. How can a client know the server they're communicating with is their intended recipient and not an imposter? What stops someone from slapping a certificate on their site with someone else's domain name on it? The answer is, as it turns out, through digital signature and Certificate Authorities.

Certificate Authorities serve as trusted third parties for the internet at large. Using rigorous verification methods, these organisations issue certificates, digitally signed by their root certificate's private key. The corresponding Certificate Authority's public key is shipped alongside Operating Systems and Web Browsers in their trusted root store. In order for the green lock icon to come up when you visit a site, your browser must be able to calculate a valid chain of trust between a root certificate of which it is already aware, and the certificate being presented by the site that you are visiting. This is an example of PKI being used to authenticate that the server you are connecting to is who they say they are. Many companies also use PKI internally for internal company authentication.

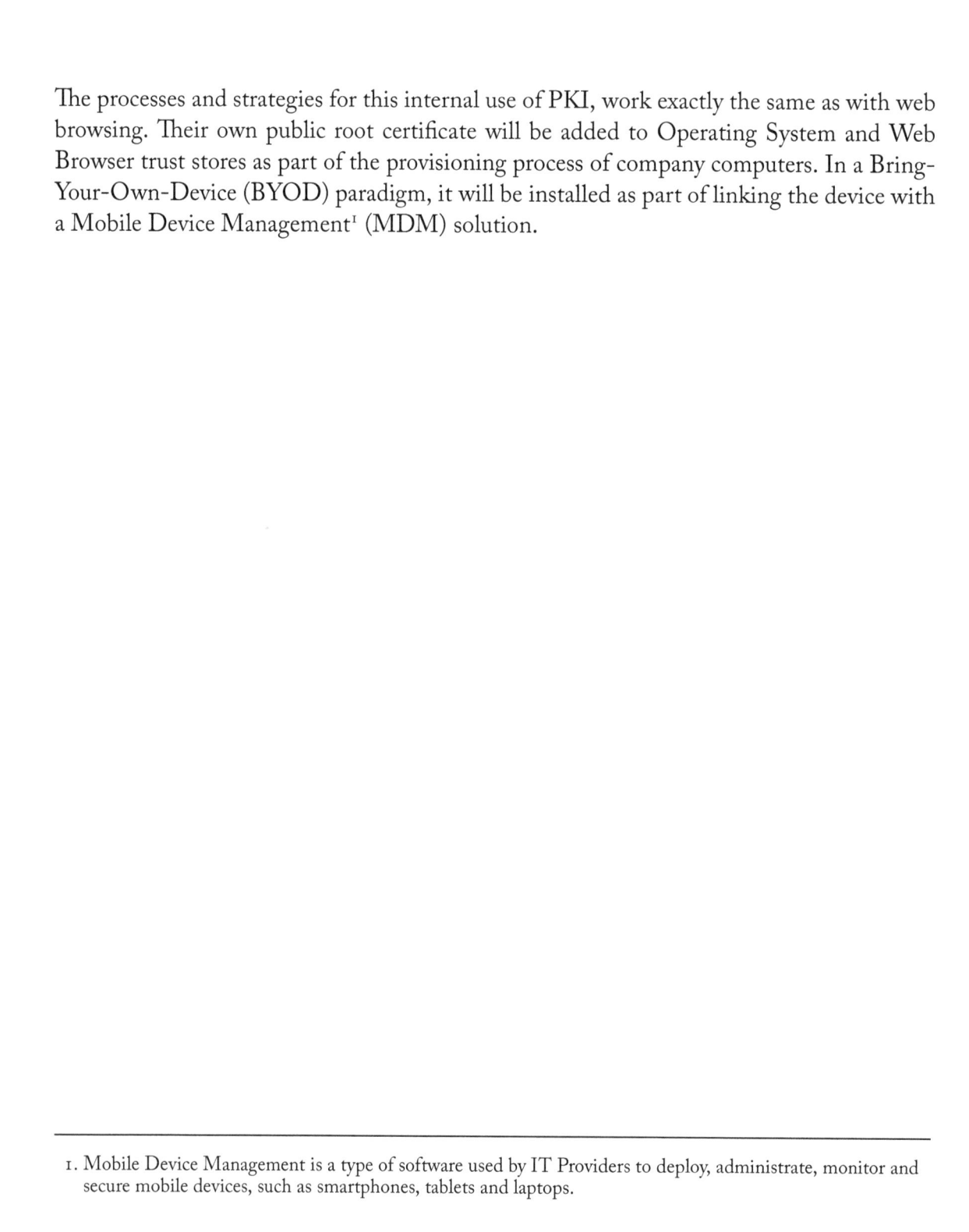

The processes and strategies for this internal use of PKI, work exactly the same as with web browsing. Their own public root certificate will be added to Operating System and Web Browser trust stores as part of the provisioning process of company computers. In a Bring-Your-Own-Device (BYOD) paradigm, it will be installed as part of linking the device with a Mobile Device Management[1] (MDM) solution.

---

[1]. Mobile Device Management is a type of software used by IT Providers to deploy, administrate, monitor and secure mobile devices, such as smartphones, tablets and laptops.

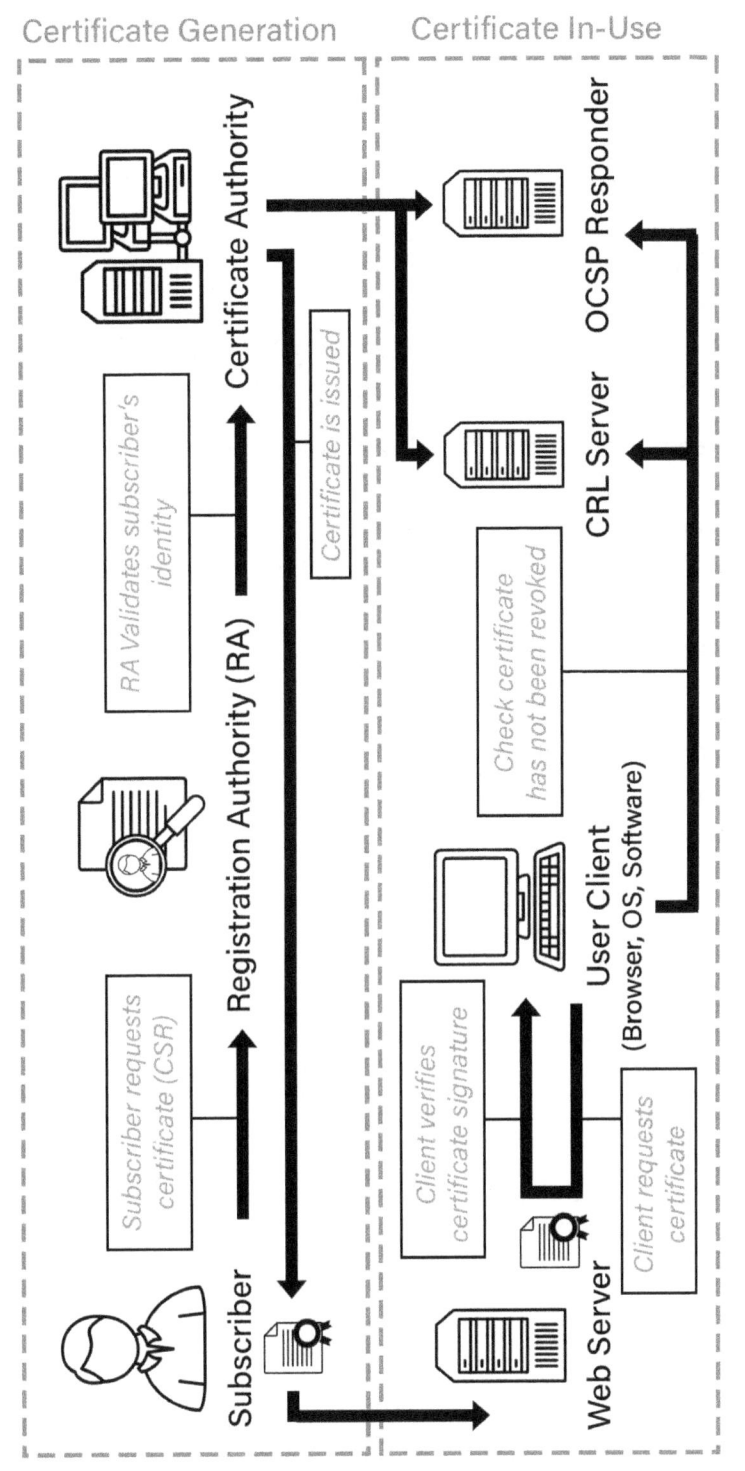

Image 3.0: Internet PKI Certificate lifecycle

Chapter 3: Public Key Infrastructure: • 41

Certificate Lifecycle

Key Pair Generation

In order to obtain a signed certificate, the first thing that needs to happen is for an administrator to generate a key pair using a key generation algorithm. In the case of SSL/TLS this usually utilises RSA encryption. As we discussed in Chapter 1: SSL/TLS, RSA key pairs are generated by selecting prime numbers at random and spitting out two keys that are intrinsically linked. To perform this calculation by hand would be rather time consuming, luckily, software such as OpenSSL (Chapter 7) can be used to perform this task.

The private key is often protected via a passphrase, since its compromise renders the encryption useless. The public key will be included in the Certificate Signing Request (CSR) that will either be self-signed, or sent to a Certificate Authority (CA) for a digital signature. The private key will never be sent to the CA, and should be kept private as the name suggests.

Certificate Signing Request:

The CSR consists of a Base64 encoded string which contains; the public key waiting to be signed, alongside various metadata about the entity requesting the certificate. It can also contain additional information that can be used for an SSL/TLS extension. Beyond the public key, the minimum amount of information required for modern browsers to trust a certificate is:

Common Name	This is the "primary" domain name for which a certificate will be valid.
Organisation	The name of the organisation requesting the certificate.
Organisational Unit	The department within the organisation requesting the certificate.
Locality	The municipality of the organisation.
Region	The full name of the state, province, or territory of the organisation.
Country Code	Two digit country code.
Subject Alternative Name	The full list of DNS names for which the certificate will be considered valid.

Table 3.0: CSR input information

The CSR is submitted to the CA, usually via a form on their website. In the case of an organisation's internal CA, they might have their own way of sending the CSR. Since the CSR contains no sensitive information, it can be safely sent via email or Instant Message.

Validation

The Certificate Authority needs to make a decision surrounding whether the request is valid or not. The degree of verification depends on the kind of certificate being requested. The most basic kind of certificate, Domain Validated (DV) Certificates, are subject to checks ensuring the party requesting the certificate has control over the domain in global DNS. Often, a Certificate Authority will provide a challenge that the domain will need to serve as a publicly available DNS TXT or CNAME record. If the CA queries TXT records at the root of the domain being validated and can see the record it requested is available, it knows the request is legitimate. Domain Validation can often also be performed via an email being sent to an approved email address under the domain, such as administrator@domain.com. Other kinds of certificates require more rigorous validation.

Issuance

Assuming that the certificate request passes muster, the Certificate Authority will append a signed hash to the digital certificate so that clients can independently verify the authenticity of the certificate. This is important, because all the client has to do is compute their own hash, decrypt the signed hash with the CA's public key they already trust, and make sure they match. This is such an inexpensive operation from a computational standpoint that it can be performed extremely quickly, even by low end mobile devices that must make the most of limited resources.

Revocation

Modern PKI provides a mechanism for a certificate to be invalidated retroactively. This is useful in the event of a private key compromise in incidences such as, a malicious attack, or the result of some kind of corporate takeover.

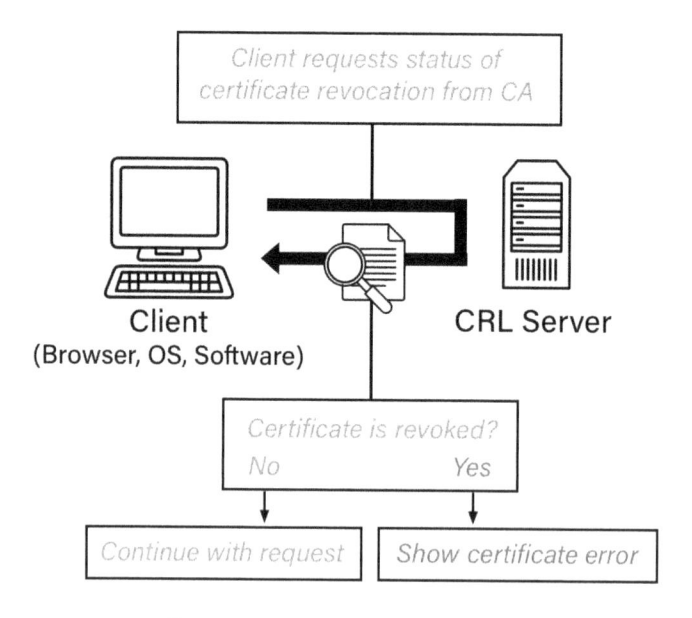

Image 3.1: Certificate revocation check

Certificate Authorities

Now that we've covered the steps in obtaining a signed certificate, it is important to understand the responsibilities the software client holds in verifying the authenticity of that certificate. Since the client is only aware of public keys from trusted Root Certificate Authorities, they must calculate a trusted path to the server. That path will always traverse at least one Root Certificate Authority, and may or may not traverse at least one Intermediate Certificate Authority. The client is also responsible for verifying that the certificate has not been revoked.

Root Certificate Authorities

A Root Certificate Authority holds a root private key and issues a self-signed public root certificate to be shipped with browsers and operating systems. Their private key is used to sign other certificates, such as node and intermediate certificates. It can also bestow upon these other certificates, privileges to operate themselves as an intermediate CA, or more commonly, just asserts that the information on the node certificate is true.

Like all certificates, root certificates have an expiration date. Keep in mind that the Root Certificate Authorities have tremendous power with their public certificates shipped in browsers. Any one of them can sign a certificate for quite literally any domain name and have it be trusted by clients everywhere.

A node certificate is also sometimes referred to as a "leaf certificate" or "end-entity certificate". These terms are used interchangeably.

Intermediate Certificate Authorities

An Intermediate Certificate Authority holds a private key which has been authorised by a Root Certificate Authority to sign node certificates. It also provides the public certificate that may be shipped with browsers or is sent to the connecting client along with the node certificate. It's called an "intermediate" certificate because it lives between the root and the node certificate in the certificate chain[2].

DigiCert High Assurance EV Root CA
Root certificate authority
Expires: Monday, 10 November 2031 at 11:00:00 am Australian Eastern Daylight Time
⊘ This certificate is valid

DigiCert SHA2 Extended Validation Server CA
Intermediate certificate authority
Expires: Sunday, 22 October 2028 at 11:00:00 pm Australian Eastern Daylight Time
⊘ This certificate is valid

digicert.com
Issued by: DigiCert SHA2 Extended Validation Server CA
Expires: Tuesday, 31 August 2021 at 10:00:00 pm Australian Eastern Standard Time
⊘ This certificate is valid

Image 3.2: Example of Certificate Chain for DigiCert

---

2. It is called a certificate "chain" because determining whether a certificate is trusted or untrusted relies upon being able to follow the signer of the certificates recursively "up the chain" until a trusted root certificate is found.

Internal Certificate Authorities

Internal Certificate Authorities do not have their root public certificates shipped with browsers or operating systems. Rather, they are pushed out by companies or governments who control the root certificate store on their own endpoint devices. By maintaining their own CA, organisations are able to decide which certificates should be trusted or revoked on their own terms. Internal Certificate Authorities are often used to secure inter-site communication between branch offices and datacenters, both on premise and in the cloud.

Certificate Cross Certification

Certificate Cross Certification is when two PKIs trust the same node certificate. For instance; if there is a hard business requirement that your server maintains compatibility with a very old version of a mobile operating system, for example one that does not support SHA-2, only SHA-1. Without certificate cross certification, your only option as an administrator would be to have all of your clients go without the added protection SHA-2 provides. With certificate cross certification, you might have the same public key signed by two Certificate Authorities and publish intermediate certificates from both. Now, the newer clients who have the SHA-2 intermediate certificates can take advantage of this protection, and the older clients will continue to function.

Another great reason to use certificate cross certification is to easily map the PKI to an organisation's hierarchy. Let's say a global organisation has a hub and spoke reporting topology. Each branch office has their own IT department, and the IT departments do not wish to trust all of each other's resources. If each IT department were to have their own CA, it would be easy for each office to cross sign resources from the other offices, in order to enforce their own organisational policy!

CRLs and OCSP Stapling

Included within the metadata sent by the CA when it signs a certificate is the location of a Certificate Revocation List (CRL). This list can be made available via HTTP, or via LDAP (Lightweight Directory Access Protocol). Although LDAP is typically not used on the internet at large, it is a popular choice for internal PKIs. Clients who support CRL functionality will make a call out to the CRL, download it, and ensure the fingerprint of the certificate they're attempting to verify does not appear on this list prior to trusting the site on behalf of the user. This is a fairly time consuming operation and at scale can put quite a burden on the server hosting the CRL.

A more recent way of providing this same feature is via OCSP (Online Certificate Status Protocol) stapling. Using this approach, the burden of proof is reversed; rather than the client needing to validate the certificate, the web server to which the client is establishing a secure connection, periodically requests information from a server run by the Certificate Authority who originally signed the certificate. The CA's server responds with a signed timestamp corresponding to the web server's last check-in, the web server then "staples" this timestamp to its own certificate. A similar analogy would be getting a stamp on your personal passport each time you visit a different country. In this second scenario, using OCSP; right from the get go, clients have the information they need to verify, both that the certificate is valid and that it has not subsequently been revoked.

Certificate Authority Authorisation (CAA)

A CAA record is a DNS record, specified by *RFC 6844*[3], that defines the policy for a domain name as to which Certificate Authorities are allowed to issue certificates for. The purpose of this CAA record is to give the power to the domain owner when it comes to who can issue certificates for the domain. If a Certificate Authority tries to issue a certificate for a domain name that does not have it listed in a CAA record, it will not be allowed to issue the certificate. It also allows the addition of a URL or EMAIL for notification by the Certificate Authorities to report any policy violations. There may be multiple CAA records on a domain to authorize multiple Certificate Authorities.

---

3. *https://www.rfc-editor.org/info/rfc6844*

The CAA record consists of 3 parts;

```
CAA <flag> <tag> <value>
```

- **Flags** are integers between 0 and 255. This is currently used to set a critical flag (set to 128) which tells any querying CA to not issue a certificate when there is a CAA record it does not understand. The default value is 0 which tells the CA to continue querying all the records if it does not understand the record.
- **Tags** can be one of 3 text values:
    - *"issue"* authorises a single CA to issue any type of certificate for the specified hostname.
    - *"issuewild"* authorises a single CA to only issue wildcard certificates for the hostname.
    - *"iodef"* is used to set a URL or email for policy violation reporting.
- **Values** are where you set the authorised CA or reporting URL for the tags. Such as the CAs "digicert.com" or "letsencrypt.org". Or for reporting you could set it as "mailto: *me@myemail.com*".

Examples:

```
CAA 0 issue "digicert.com"
```

This will allow digicert to issue certificates for the domain name.

```
CAA 0 issuewild "digicert.com"

CAA 0 issue "letsencrypt.com"

CAA 0 iodef "mailto: me@mydomain.com"
```

This will allow digicert to only issue wildcard certificates and letsencrypt to issue any other certificates. If a Certificate Authority wants to report any policy violations, they can email me@mydomain.com.

If no CAA record is found when a CA queries the domain's DNS. It is allowed to issue a certificate for the domain.

Most Utilized and Publicly Trusted Certificate Authorities

The list below contains the most common publicly trusted Certificate Authorities used on public facing websites.

Certificate Authority	Market Share
IdenTrust	51.5%
DigiCert Group	19.6%
Sectigo	17.4%
GoDaddy Group	6.9%
GlobalSign	3.0%
Certum	0.6%
Secom Trust	0.2%
Entrust	0.2%
Other (Each representing under 0.1%)	0.6%

Table 3.1: Statistics obtained from (w3techs.com, 15th May 2020): https://w3techs.com/technologies/overview/ssl_certificate

If you are looking to obtain an SSL/TLS certificate signed by a trusted Certificate Authority, SSLTrust is a great place to start: https://www.ssltrust.com.au/

CHAPTER 4

X.509 Certificates

X.509 certificates are a standard specification for public keys and their respective metadata. They were defined in 1988 by the International Telecommunications Standardisation Sector; ITU-T.

When anyone is talking about SSL/TLS Certificates, they will essentially be talking about X.509 Certificates. When a client browser connects to a server and receives the Certificate containing the public key, it will be with the X.509 format.

They are used for (but not limited to):

- SSL/TLS and HTTPS
- Code Signing
- Document Signing
- Client Authentication
- Government-issued Electronic ID

Certificate Fields

Version	The specific revision of the X.509 protocol being adhered to.
Serial Number	An identifier unique to the certificate relative only to the issuing body. (Not globally unique).
Algorithm	The algorithm used to sign the certificate.
Issuer Name	The distinguished name is a fully qualified name defining the authority signing the certificate.
Validity Period	The date the certificate is issued until the date it expires, expressed as a range.
Subject Name	The distinguished name is a fully qualified name defining the entity the certificate is issued to.
Public Key	The public portion of the asymmetric key being signed.
Extensions	A list of extensions for which the Certificate Authority is also authorizing.

Table 4.0: X.509 Certificate Fields

www.google.com
Issued by: GTS CA 1O1
Expires: Tuesday, 28 July 2020 at 6:31:24 pm Australian Eastern Standard Time
✓ This certificate is valid

▶ Trust
▼ Details

Subject Name
Country or Region US
State/Province California
Locality Mountain View
Organisation Google LLC
Common Name www.google.com

Issuer Name
Country or Region US
Organisation Google Trust Services
Common Name GTS CA 1O1

Serial Number 3B E4 0F 3B F6 41 86 B6 02 00 00 00 00 67 33 09
Version 3
Signature Algorithm SHA-256 with RSA Encryption (1.2.840.113549.1.1.11)
Parameters None

Not Valid Before Tuesday, 5 May 2020 at 6:31:24 pm Australian Eastern Standard Time
Not Valid After Tuesday, 28 July 2020 at 6:31:24 pm Australian Eastern Standard Time

Public Key Info
Algorithm Elliptic Curve Public Key (1.2.840.10045.2.1)
Parameters Elliptic Curve secp256r1 (1.2.840.10045.3.1.7)
Public Key 65 bytes : 04 9C 54 28 65 13 7F 39 …
Key Size 256 bits
Key Usage Encrypt, Verify, Derive

Signature 256 bytes : CE 9E BF 31 44 C2 5A 57 …

Image 4.0: Google's X.509 Certificate

Certificate Extensions

Like many of the protocols that have stood the test of time, X.509 recognized the need to support changing requirements. Extensions provide a mechanism for systems to include agreed upon strings of arbitrary, trusted data for consumption by computing systems. For example, *RFC 5280*[1] defines a way for a Certificate Authority to stamp a certificate with its certification revocation information, when it signs the certificate. Of course, for this information to be useful, both the authority signing the certificate and the client consuming the certificate must be aware of what a specific extension is, and how to safely parse its value. To facilitate this, a certificate extension is not a key value pair as you might expect, rather, it is a 3-tuple consisting of; the extension name, the extension value, and a boolean flag that dictates whether the extension is marked 'critical'. Extensions marked 'critical' require the client to either recognize the extension and how to process it, or throw an error. Unrecognized extensions without the critical bit set can be safely ignored by the application, and trusted regardless, as best as the application knows how. Different combinations of extensions lend themselves to different purposes. This is explored next in "types of certificates".

Type of Certificates

Really, all certificates are the same. We give them different names as a shorthand to describe what combinations of options make the certificate suitable for different purposes.

Standard

When talking about SSL/TLS certificates (which as we know are really X.509 certificates), most of the time we're talking about a certificate authorised by a CA for "server authentication" usage. This kind of certificate is valid for a particular domain name.

---

[1]. *https://www.rfc-editor.org/info/rfc5280*

Wildcard Certificates

Wildcard Certificates are special in that they are valid for an entire subdomain space. They provide businesses with flexibility. However, this flexibility comes with a trade off. Since they are valid for that entire subdomain there is a potential risk of increased damage should the private key become compromised.

Wildcard certificates are really useful when an organisation does not necessarily know which subdomains they need secured upfront. Often, a single wildcard certificate will be loaded onto a reverse proxy (also referred to as a "middlebox", see Chapter 5: Proxies/Middleboxes), and re-terminate SSL/TLS connections to a backing server. The backing server's certificate is an excellent candidate for an internally trusted PKI.

Wildcard certificates are populated with an * for the subdomain in either the Common Name (CN) field, or the Subject Alternative Name (SAN) field of a certificate. (Technically, the latter is also an example of a SAN certificate, and different software may or may not support either scenario). It's important to keep in mind that there is no such thing as a "double wildcard" — wildcard domains are only valid with one wildcard subdomain space/level. A SAN certificate however, can contain multiple wildcard domains!

For example, a wildcard certificate with the Common Name *.example.com would cover test.example.com, www.example.com and mail.example.com but not my.page.example.com (because it is two levels deep). A multi-domain wildcard however, could have *.example.com and *.page.example.com in the SAN field of the certificate in order to cover all of the above scenarios. What is NOT possible is for a certificate to contain *.*.example.com — this is an invalid configuration.

Valid WIldcard SAN/Common Names	Invalid Wildcard SAN/Common Names
*.domain.com	www.*.domain.com
*.sub.domain.com	*.*.domain.com
*.sub2.sub.domain.com	*.sub2.*.domain.com

Table 4.1: Valid Wildcard Domains

SAN/UCC Certificates

Subject Alternative Name (SAN) certificates allow for multiple DNS names to be valid under the same certificate. This is accomplished by including multiple Common Names in the SAN field of the certificate as a list. There are no restrictions on which domains can be included within this certificate. However, the CA will have to verify each one independently and either approve or deny the CSR as a unit. (They will not approve a certificate for only some of the requested domains, a new CSR would have to be submitted). SAN certificates are an excellent balance of security and flexibility. They are perfect for when an organisation has a lot of domains that need to be secured, but new domains are not added with regularity.

Unified Communications Certificates (UCC Certificates) are really just SAN certificates with some additional stipulated requirements by Microsoft, for use with Exchange Server. Specifically, Microsoft Exchange requires the short name of servers to be trusted by the certificate (not just the FQDN[2]). It is important for the SAN field to contain a complete list of valid domains (Exchange will not concatenate the CN field and the SAN field). Finally, the certificate must support the Certificate Revocation List extension and provide a CRL distribution endpoint.

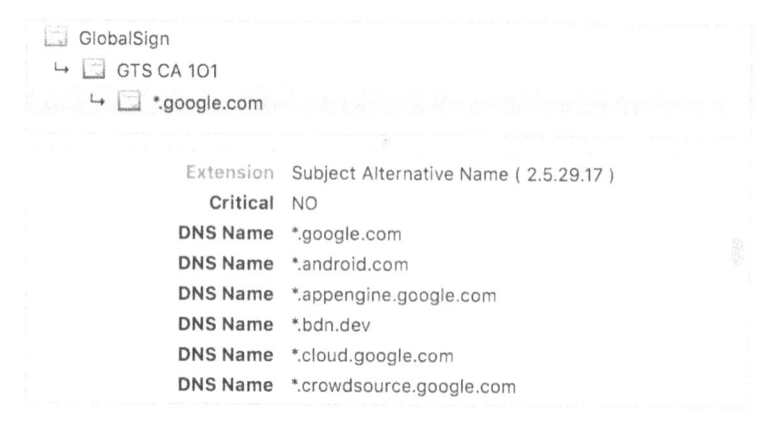

```
GlobalSign
 └─ GTS CA 101
     └─ *.google.com

    Extension  Subject Alternative Name ( 2.5.29.17 )
    Critical   NO
    DNS Name   *.google.com
    DNS Name   *.android.com
    DNS Name   *.appengine.google.com
    DNS Name   *.bdn.dev
    DNS Name   *.cloud.google.com
    DNS Name   *.crowdsource.google.com
```

Image 4.1: SAN list in Google's Certificate

---

2. Fully Qualified Domain Names are a complete domain name containing both the host name (subdomains) and the root domain.

Client Certificates

Client certificates are used to authenticate a client to the server, and used relatively rarely. When used in conjunction with server certificates, this is referred to as "mutual authentication". In this configuration, a certificate uniquely identifying the client is issued (usually by an internal PKI). The server only allows access to clients that present a certificate from the CA they are configured to trust. Without a valid certificate, the server will drop the connection. Once authenticated, the server can use the CN in the client certificate as the username for the user inside the application. This provides a seamless user experience, and is often used by companies with managed devices in order to authenticate internal resources with as little friction for the end user as possible.

In Bring-Your-Own-Device (BYOD) implementations, the mobile device management (MDM) software solution is usually responsible for handing out a certificate to the endpoint during initial provisioning. Sometimes, reverse proxies will use client authentication, but still require the end user to sign-in to the backing application. This is a form of multi-factor authentication, and is popular with governments and business to business (B2B) portals.

Code Signing Certificates

Code Signing Certificates are used to sign binaries during compile time. This allows an end user to trust that software hasn't been modified to include malicious code after the code's author has compiled it. Code signing certificates that meet Microsoft's requirements are referred to as "Authenticode Certificates". Analogously, certificates trusted by Apple must meet the stipulations of "Apple Code Signing Certificates". At its heart though, a Code Signing Certificate is simply a certificate trusted by a CA to sign the hash of an arbitrary binary.

An interesting question raised by the need for code signing certificates is, what should happen when a code signing certificate expires? It would be unfortunate if code that was working and trusted simply stopped working. To combat this, CAs which issue code signing certificates will host Time Stamping Servers. These time stamping servers simply provide an attestation from the certificate issuer as to when a certificate was used to sign an executable. Executables with a valid timestamp will continue to be trusted as long as it was signed during the certificates validity window, even if that validity window has since expired.

CHAPTER 5

Vulnerabilities and Flaws

In the news we frequently hear about new discoveries of weaknesses in various encryption strategies. It truly is a moving target. Much of effective encryption relies upon what is beyond the power of today's computers to calculate.

When assessing the strength of SSL/TLS used in a particular way, there are a surprisingly large number of things that, if compromised, could lead to the decryption of sensitive information. The next time you see an attack mentioned in the news, see if you can figure out which of the items below is being abused.

Key Size

As we learned in chapter 1, SSL/TLS relies on both asymmetric and symmetric cryptography. The key generation algorithms used in both of these systems take a particular key size. The Key Size is the length of the key which is expressed in; number of bits. It directly correlates to the number of possible keys, which in turn is referred to as the "key space". For example; a Key Size of 2048 bits would result in a key space of 2^{2048}, this equates to an enormous number of possible keys (over 3.2×10^{616})

If one were to attempt to decrypt the ciphertext with each and every possible key, by definition, the message will eventually be successfully decrypted. This kind of attack is referred to as a "brute force" attack. RSA keys for example, are considered reasonably secure at 2048 bits in size, since the resulting number of combinations would be so numerous that today's computers attempting a brute force attack of guess and check, would take longer to compute than the lifetime of anyone on the planet right now. Why then do we not simply pick an absurdly long key and call it a day? Well, longer keys require additional computing power in order to both encrypt and decrypt. This process consumes massive power on mobile devices and greatly affects communications speeds, so it's imperative to find the right balance of speed and security.

MITM Attack

A Man-In-The-Middle attack refers to someone intercepting traffic on the wire between the server and the client. This kind of attack can take many forms. An attacker could be listening on the local subnet of the server or client. They could even have tapped into a carrier fibre line at a telephone pole. It's possible they could have set up their own server and used malicious code, running it on the endpoint to inject something into the computer's ARP cache or routing table. Luckily, SSL/TLS addresses all of these scenarios, except for one. Can you guess which?

SSL/TLS cannot protect against malicious code running on your own desktop. (Think about it — an attacker with control of your machine could trust arbitrary root certificates and send your traffic to them instead of the server you're trying to communicate with.) Therefore, short of machine compromise, MITM attacks usually rely on an additional vulnerability to be effective. For example, if communication occurs using a weak keysize, the attacker could take the traffic they've gathered via MITM and brute force it!

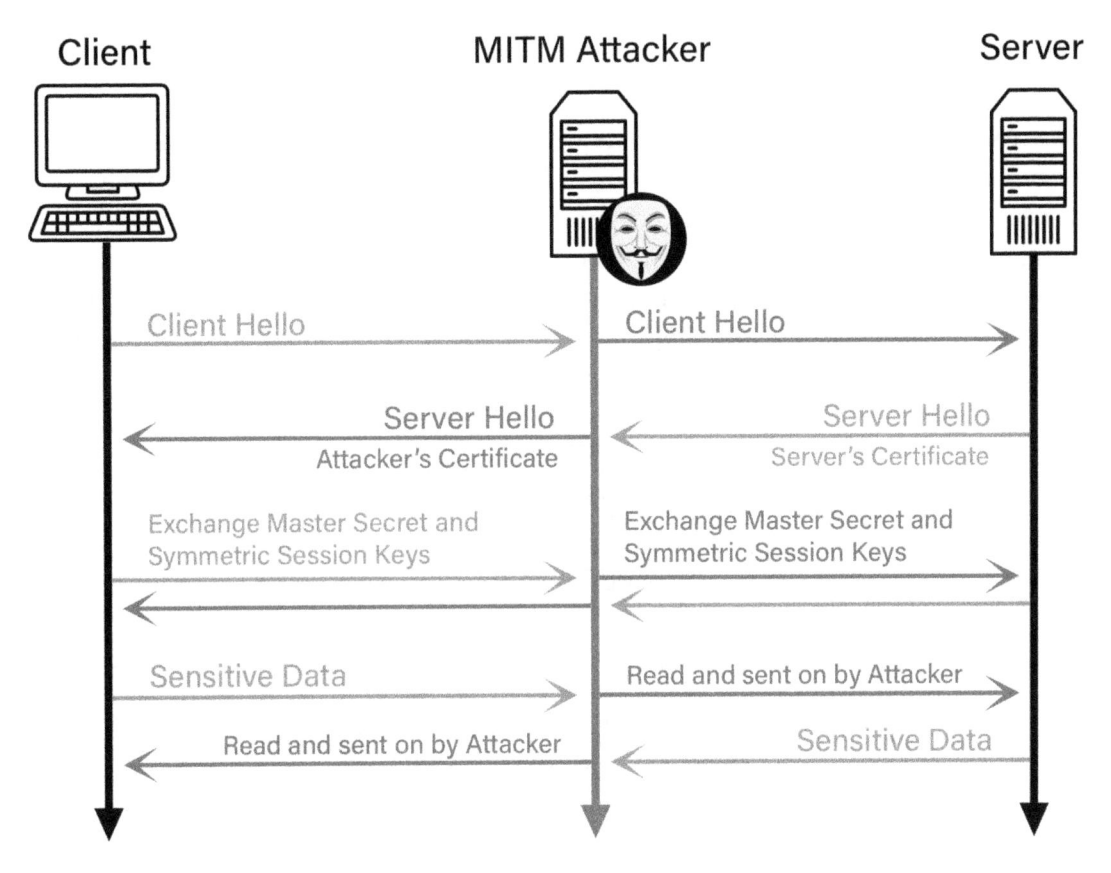

Image 5.0: MITM Attack

Upstream Compromise

Upstream compromise refers to the very real possibility of a crucial component of SSL/TLS being broken without your knowledge. These sort of doomsday scenarios include; a CA losing control of their private keys, a computer manufacturer being compromised at the hardware or firmware level, or even the specific server that you are communicating with being compromised without your knowledge.

Key Escrow

Key Escrow is a very controversial practice whereby private keys are held by a trusted third party in the event of emergency situations. This has been proposed by multiple government agencies as a means of eavesdropping on digital communications in the course of legal investigations. At first blush this doesn't sound like a bad thing, but there is no technically feasible way to create a backdoor that only the good guys can use. Key Escrow inherently introduces unreasonable risk into cryptographic systems. It is sometimes used by an internal PKI for deployments where less security is required.

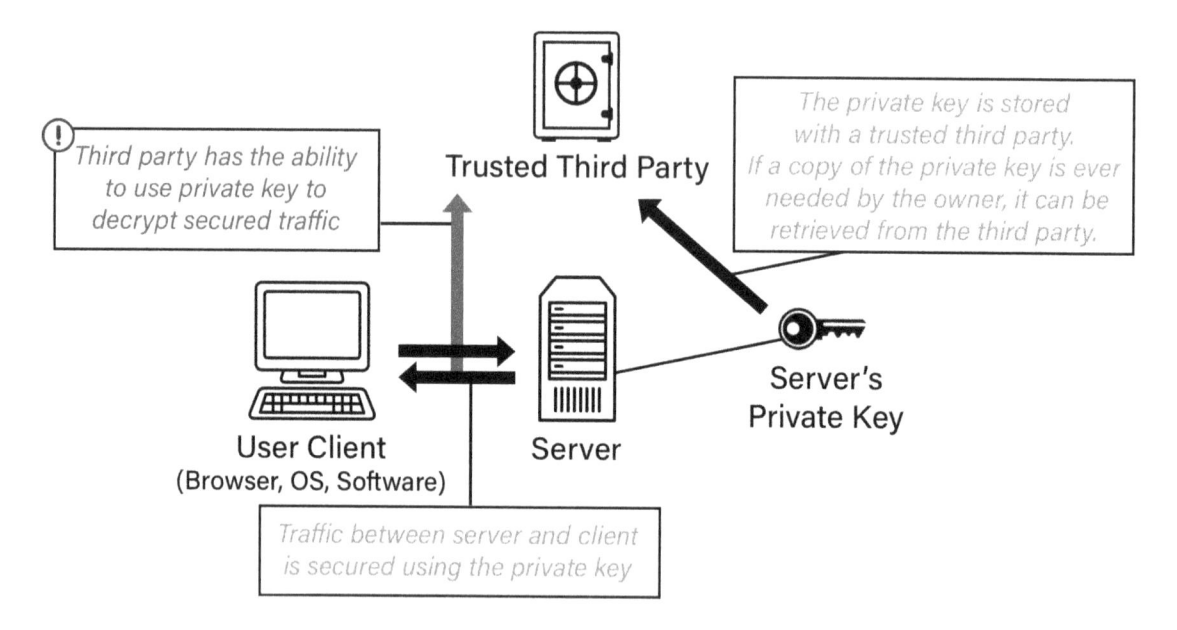

Image 5.1: Private Key Storage with Third Party

Proxies/Middleboxes

When it comes to SSL/TLS, there are multiple kinds of proxies. These can be first subdivided into non-terminating and terminating proxies. A non-terminating proxy operates at layer 4 of the OSI model, and simply forwards along TCP traffic to another host for processing. A much more concerning type of proxy is a terminating proxy. This proxy acts as a MITM, and actually decrypts traffic before deciding what to do with it. It can either pass the traffic along over plaintext (unencrypted), or re-encrypt a new connection to talk with the backing server.

Why would an organization choose to use proxies or middleboxes? The answer lies with an organisation's priorities. You cannot interrogate what you cannot read, and many industries rely on "deep packet inspection" to protect against the threat of digital theft. Imagine if an employee, on their way out the door, could send themselves company secrets. Without DPI, using an SSL/TLS connection only, would thwart a company's attempts to track this and sue the departing employee for it.

Digital Signature Forgery

The CA's digital signature allows browsers to make trust decisions. Digital signatures rely on one-way functions to provide message integrity and non-repudiation. In a perfect cryptosystem, only the compromise of the root CA's private key would allow a bad actor to impersonate the Certificate Authority. However, a digital signature is only as strong as its one-way function. As of fairly recently, SHA-1 has been considered unsuitable for digital signatures due to modern computers becoming more and more powerful. When an attacker attempts to create an arbitrary message which has the same computational hash as another valid message, this is referred to as a "collision attack". If an attacker can construct a message that browsers hash to the same value as the valid signed certificate, the attacker doesn't even need the CA's private key to trick the browser into trusting it. (Padding, and a lot of guess and check, is used to create these collision messages.)

SSL Stripping

Many websites, in order to provide compatibility for older clients, are accessible over both HTTP and HTTPS. Even more will provide an HTTP to HTTPS redirect to make it easier for users to access the site. These redirects are inherently a security risk, because of SSL Stripping. SSL Stripping occurs when an attacker targets this initial communication over HTTP. By intercepting the content in-transit over this unsecured protocol, the attacker can then modify further communication by maintaining a HTTP connection with the user and themselves connecting securely over HTTPS to the server In this scenario, they don't even have to compromise SSL/TLS in order to snoop.

Well-Known Attacks

Over the years, a number of vulnerabilities have stood out as particularly notable. These are useful to study in order to understand the moving pieces of a secure system. The ground is moving under us as computers advance at a breakneck pace. What was secure just a few years ago may not cut the mustard today. Vulnerabilities against SSL/TLS can be categorized with a broad stroke into two categories: those which are specific to a particular software implementation (fixable) and those which are an inherent flaw in the standard itself (unfixable). For example, an implementation flaw may exist in OpenSSL[1] and yet be fixed in the next release. It may or may not also be present in LibreSSL. A protocol flaw on the other hand, cannot be fixed without crafting a new standard for the software to adhere to.

A useful tool to test for vulnerabilities in a publicly accessible SSL/TLS installation can be found here: https://www.ssltrust.com/ssl-tools/website-security-check and https://www.ssllabs.com/ssltest/

---

[1]. OpenSSL and LibreSSL are a software libraries for applications to implement SSL/TLS communications

POODLE

POODLE[2] (Padding Oracle On Downgraded Legacy Encryption) is an attack that slowly reconstructs the plaintext of a message by making inferences based on the server's error response. Malicious Javascript running in the client's browser repeatedly makes these requests by strategically padding the request with nonsense. This results in the bit they're trying to decode occurring in the right location, eventually piecing together the plaintext in its entirety. POODLE is a protocol flaw, and was unable to be corrected in SSL 3.0. Later, a similar attack (also referred to as POODLE) affected TLS 1.0 in certain configurations.

Heartbleed

Heartbleed[3] is an example of a "buffer overread" attack. By sending specially crafted messages, an attacker is able to trick the server into responding; not just with what it's supposed to respond with, but also with several additional bits of whatever happened to be in recent memory. By repeatedly sending requests to "prime the buffer" an attacker can piece together plaintext a little at a time. Unlike POODLE, heartbleed is an implementation flaw, and was patched in OpenSSL 1.0.1.g. This led to a mass scrambling to update affected versions. Software that dynamically links against the libraries it relies upon (at runtime) was easy to patch by updating the library as a package in the Operating System's package manager. Software which statically links dependencies (links at compile time) was much more difficult to fix. The developer had to release a new version of the software. Since that time, many organizations (rightfully) treat statically linked dependencies as a business risk when evaluating new software.

---

2. *https://security.googleblog.com/2014/10/this-poodle-bites-exploiting-ssl-30.html*
3. *https://en.wikipedia.org/wiki/Heartbleed*

DROWN

DROWN[4] (Decrypting RSA using Obsolete and Weakened Encryption) is a protocol level flaw in SSL 2.0 that allows an attacker to obtain a server's private key, and with this, decrypt all communication going forwards and backwards. What makes this even worse, is that because the private key is the same no matter which protocol version clients support, if a server supports (or ever supported) SSL 2.0 and a bad actor happened to obtain its private key, even traffic using strong TLS can be compromised. This holds true even for traffic on a totally different server where that private key was reused. DROWN illustrates the need for securely handling key material.

CRIME, and BREACH

CRIME[5] (Compression Ratio Infoleak Made Easy) and BREACH (Browser Reconnaissance and Exfiltration via Adaptive Compression of Hypertext) are two extremely similar attacks that abuse compression. CRIME works against TLS compression while *BREACH*[6] compromises HTTP compression. For TLS compression to work correctly, it must be supported by both the server and the client as a TLS extension. Disabling TLS compression, either client side or server side, stops CRIME in its tracks. Later, reasonable mitigations were introduced that allowed TLS compression in certain non-vulnerable circumstances. BREACH however, is trickier, because HTTP compression happens inside the protocol traversing the already presumed secure tunnel. This type of attack is so devastating that, even after mitigations have been introduced, many administrators prudently forego HTTP compression altogether.

---

4. *https://drownattack.com/drown-attack-paper.pdf*
5. *https://arstechnica.com/information-technology/2012/09/crime-hijacks-https-sessions/*
6. *https://en.wikipedia.org/wiki/BREACH*

Targeted Nationstate Attacks

An attack carried out by an entity with sufficient resources is impossible to defend against. When working with millions or billions of dollars, highly secret prototype hardware and a country's very best minds, we cannot know for certain that a particular government or corporation hasn't completely compromised the assumptions which SSL/TLS relies upon. In most situations, this is simply an acceptable risk. The vast majority of companies are interested only in exercising due diligence and due care in order to not breach their fiduciary duties.

Quantum Computing

Quantum computers are likely to turn modern encryption on its head. Unlike classical computers, Quantum computers do not work with 0's and 1's as their primary building blocks. Quantum computers leverage what's called the superposition of 0's and 1's, to represent state in an entirely new way. They are not expected to be general purpose machines. They are not an "evolution" of classical computers, and they are not "faster" in the sense that you'll be able to browse the internet faster or have better battery life. Instead, they are good at solving incredibly specific problems. It just so happens that one of these problems is the factorization of large prime numbers — the very foundational assumption behind RSA and AES. As of 2019, both Google and IBM have working prototypes of quantum computers (that do not yet scale to the level of breaking RSA). Overnight however, this could change, and the race will be on to come up with better encryption strategies before this technology trickles down to the commodity market. The NIST estimates that RSA-2048 will be broken in "as early as 15 years".

You can read more on the NIST Post Quantum Cryptography Project here: https://csrc.nist.gov/projects/post-quantum-cryptography

CHAPTER 6

Implementation

Up until this point, we've mostly discussed the standards and specifications required for SSL/TLS to be a secure cryptosystem. In this chapter we deep dive into the nitty gritty, with each section representing a decision. Some of these decisions were made when a web server or an operating system were written. Other decisions are left up to the person configuring the server. Still more of these decisions have evolved over time. SSL/TLS is a topic that is often seen as confusing, especially for the beginner. If there is a chapter in this book that is worth reading twice, it is this one. Commit these things to memory, and you will have a leg up on many seasoned administrators.

A Plethora of File Formats and Extensions

All implementations of SSL/TLS require a public and a private key. That private key needs to be secured somewhere. It also needs to be located where it is accessible to the server software that requires access to it. There are a surprisingly large number of ways these files are stored.

Base64 or Binary?

The two most common formats by far are Base64 encoded certificates, and Binary certificates. A Base64 encoded certificate is simply encoded ASCII text. A Base64 certificate structures this text according to the PEM format, as defined by the IETF in *RFC 7486*[1]. A Binary certificate is a certificate encoded with a method called DER, as described by ASN.1[2]. Base64 certificates can be manipulated in a text editor, while Binary certificates require a computer program capable of understanding a binary stream.

The first question you should always ask yourself when working with a new software that uses SSL/TLS keys is whether the key files are stored in Base64 or Binary. Passing a Binary certificate to software that is expecting a Base64 certificate, or vice versa, will result in difficult to understand errors. You can easily convert between the two formats with something like OpenSSL (Chapter 7). To identify if a certificate file is Base64 or Binary, open it in a text editor, such as notepad.

If the certificate is Base64 you will see characters between two tags:

`-----BEGIN CERTIFICATE-----` and `-----END CERTIFICATE-----`

A Binary certificate however, will not have these tags. Even without opening the file, it may be possible to determine the certificate type. If you see a file with the extension .PEM, .CRT, .KEY, or .P7B, it is almost undoubtedly a Base64 encoded certificate. If you see the file extensions .DER, .CER, .PFX or .P12 it is almost certainly Binary encoded.

---

1. *https://www.rfc-editor.org/info/rfc7486*
2. ASN.1 is a language for describing data structures used frequently when designing computer protocols.

Base64

PEM	PKCS#7
.pem .crt .key .csr .ca-bundle	.p7b .p7s .p7c

Binary

DER	PKCS#12
.der .cer	.pfx .p12

Table 6.0: File Formats

Public Key, Private Key, or both?

The next question you should be asking is whether a file contains the public key, the private key, or the whole key pair. This is very important to ascertain. While you may very well email someone your public key, you must never share your private key under any circumstances! The file extensions .CRT, .CER, .DER, .CER and .P7B by convention will include only public keys. The extension .KEY will contain private keys. The extension .PEM may include either public or private keys, so be very careful with it. The extension .pfx will contain both public and private keys according to the format PKCS#12, so be very careful when copying these files. Windows typically uses .CRT files in the PKCS#7 format for public certificates, and .pfx files that contain both the public and private key. Unlike *nix systems, there is no mechanism for working with only a private key.

Private Key	Public Key or Certificate Signing Request
.pem* .p12 .pfx .key	.crt .cer .der .p7b .csr

Table: Table 6.1: Key File Formats
May not contain a private key, but treat it as if it does until you're 100% certain.

Windows SCHANNEL

Windows implementation of SSL/TLS is handled by the provider "SCHANNEL" (Secure Channel). SCHANNEL refers to part of the Operating System which is responsible for handling SSL/TLS. SCHANNEL works with the low level Microsoft CryptoAPI in order to expose SSL/TLS related operations to .NET for consumption by .NET developers. The CryptoAPI handles encryption and decryption, hashes and digital signatures and code signing certificates. Basically, if it's a topic we are discussing in this book, Microsoft implements it using SCHANNEL and the CryptoAPI.

Java Keystores

JAVA is a popular high-level programming language whose huge draw is that code written in JAVA is platform agnostic. JAVA compiles to an intermediate format called JVM bytecode. This byte code is an instruction set for a virtual machine that can run on Windows, OSX or *nix variants. Because this virtual machine runs transparently on top of its host, it has its own quirks and conventions.

One of those conventions is its own key storage format. Java stores public and private keys inside of the JKS (Java Keystore). The JKS exists as a file with the extension .JKS, but the file is more like a database than a flat file. It can be manipulated using a program called KeyTool bundled with Java, or via a handful of third party GUI utilities. Java typically has two JKS keystores that you will need to be concerned with —the one containing application certificates, which does not have a standard name, and the other containing its root certificate store, always called CACerts and located in JRE/LIB/Security, relative to wherever JAVA is installed on your platform.

*nix Conventions

Typically, Linux and Unix systems will use Base64 encoded public and private keys. Most typically, you'll see a .PEM extension. Intermediate certificates are either specified separately, or concatenated together in a file with the extension .BUNDLE.

PKCS #7 and PKCS #12

PKCS #7 refers to *RFC 2315*[3], and describes a popular format for formatting a public key. PKCS #12, described by *RFC 7292*[4], describes a format for formatting a public and private key together in the same file. In the Windows world, the binary .PFX is a PKCS12, and the binary .CER is a PKCS7.

A .BUNDLE is simply the full chain (minus the root certificate, which is redundant to include). It is ordered from highest to lowest with the intermediate chaining directly to a root on top, followed by any intermediates between your leaf certificate and that first intermediate, and concludes with your leaf certificate.

Private Key Storage

HSMs

A Hardware Security Module (HSM) is a third party device (usually rack mountable) whose job is to manage secure storage of the sensitive private key material across your infrastructure. Via proprietary APIs and client-side agents, HSMs ensure that even a compromise of your infrastructure does not result in theft of your private keys. HSMs are the gold standard in terms of security, but also, introduce additional complexity and higher cost. Due to this, you'll usually only see HSMs in larger environments.

DPAPI

Windows Data Protection API (DPAPI) is the underlying OS construct responsible for storage of private keys on a Windows System. Accessible to be managed through the Certificates MMC Snapin, private keys are securely stored in a "certificate store", and symmetrically encrypted by a service principal's private key. There are 3 options when selecting a certificate store: "Computer" contains keys accessible to be used via DPAPI on the current computer, "User" stores keys for the current user, and "Service Account", which allows you to select an account that runs software on your system.

Unless a key has specifically been marked as "Exportable" when imported into the certificate store (or created via the MMC), Windows will not export this key to the file system.

---

3. *https://www.rfc-editor.org/info/rfc2315*
4. *https://www.rfc-editor.org/info/rfc7292*

The key is only recoverable by forensic analysis of the computer's running memory for the process space configured to use the key. It is considered a very secure way of storing private keys.

File System ACLs

Linux and Unix systems tend to rely on file system permissions for securing private keys.

The default permission scheme on *nix systems are commonly referred to as "Owner Group World", though modern systems can also be configured to use Access Control Lists (ACLs). It might seem odd to dive deep into Unix permissions in a book about SSL/TLS, but this book is geared towards enabling the absolute beginner to be able to bootstrap themselves into a practical understanding. If you cannot configure unix-style permissions, you cannot securely configure a server.

Every file and folder on a *nix system has a permission set defined. This permission set is a 3x3 array of bits.

	Owner	Group	World
Read	400	040	004
Write	200	020	002
Execute	100	010	001
	Only Root can access the file with the permission set to 000		

Table 6.2: File and Folder Permissions

These permissions are then encoded in a 3 digit base-8 number called "Octal Notation". (We use octal because it works out that there's no possible number higher than 7 in this scheme. Really, we're looking at 3 numbers, each with possible values 0-7).

Execute is assigned a value of 1. Write is assigned a value of 2. Read is assigned a value of 4. Owner is assigned a multiplier of 100. Group is assigned a multiplier of 10. World is assigned a multiplier of 1.

To calculate an octal for a given situation add up the assigned values in table 6.2.

For example:

- If we want the owner to be able read, write and execute (400 + 200 + 100 = 700).
- And we want the group to be able to read and write (040 + 020 = 060).
- With everyone else having no access at all (000).

Then we add up all the values, in this case resulting in a value of 760

777 is the least restrictive permission set. This grants read, write, and execute to user, group, and world.

755 is a very common octal, used to grant the owner of a file read, write, execute but grant everyone else only read and execute.

Let's say we're configuring Apache or Nginx, both of which use the www-data account by default.

First, set the ownership of your private key to the www-data user and the www-data group.

For private keys, we most commonly use octal 700 (read/write/execute to the owner, and no permissions to anyone else).

```
chown www-data:www-data /some/location/key.pem
```

Now we set the permissions.

```
chmod 700 /some/location/key.pem
```

CHAPTER 7

OpenSSL

OpenSSL[1] is one of the most popular libraries for working with public and private keys. Written in C, it provides abstractions of low-level cryptographic functions and is available for both Windows, Mac and *nix systems. On Windows, you can either compile it yourself, or find a trusted source for pre-compiled binaries. On Linux, the experience is much easier: simply install the package from your system's package manager.

It is important to note however, that not all software which uses OpenSSL relies on it being installed at the Operating System level. Indeed, most software will bundle a statically compiled version of OpenSSL within it. This means that if a vulnerability in OpenSSL is discovered, you will need to seek a new version of the software from the package maintainer. Patching your system is not enough!

---

1. *https://www.openssl.org/*

Setup and Using OpenSSL

Windows

OpenSSL can be compiled with either Visual Studio or the Borland compiler (Compiling your own OpenSSL package is beyond the scope of this book). The OpenSSL project provides a list of sources from which to download a pre-compiled binary. None of these sources are from major players in the field nor are they guaranteed to be trusted.

Another setup option would be to run a Linux distribution inside a VM, we recommend *https://www.virtualbox.org*. If you accrue enough of them, we also recommend Vagrant: *https://www.vagrantup.com* for managing your workflow.

Mac

On OSX, OpenSSL can be built from source in XCode or installed using a third party package manager such as MacPorts or Homebrew.

Install MacPorts: *https://www.macports.org/*

Open the Terminal app and type:

```
sudo /opt/local/bin/port -N install openssl +universal
```

Another option would be to run a Linux distribution inside a VM. We recommend VirtualBox: *https://www.virtualbox.org/*

Linux

On RedHat based systems, YUM is the default package manager.

`yum install openssl` will install the latest version of OpenSSL currently available in your Operating System's current repositories.

On Debian based systems, Apt-Get is the default package manager.

`apt-get install openssl` will install the latest version of OpenSSL currently available in your Operating System's current repositories.

Common Commands

The following commands all generate files in your current directory. Use the `cd` command to change into a different directory. Alternatively, the full path of a file can be substituted for the ./ syntax.

Generating a Self Signed Certificate:

```
openssl req -x509 -sha256 -nodes -days 365 -newkey rsa:2048 -keyout ./private.key -out ./certificate.crt
```

Generating a CSR for third party signature:

```
openssl req -out ./myCSR.csr -new -newkey rsa:2048 -nodes -keyout ./myKey.key
```

Converting a Binary certificate into a Base64 certificate:

```
openssl x509 -inform der -in ./binaryCertificate.der -out ./base64Certificate.pem
```

Converting a Base64 certificate into a Binary certificate:

```
openssl x509 -outform der -in ./base64Certificate.pem -out ./binaryCertificate.der
```

Splitting a PKCS12 (PFX) into its component public and private keys:

```
openssl pkcs12 -in Keypair.pfx -nocerts -nodes -out ./mykey.key
```

```
openssl pkcs12 -in Keypair.pfx -clcerts -nokeys -out ./mycert.pem
```

Combining a Base64 public and private key into a PKCS12 (PFX):

```
openssl pkcs12 -export -out Keypair.pfx -inkey ./private.key -in ./certificate.crt -certfile ./intermediates.crt
```

In the above command, the `-certfile` parameter is optional depending on if you have intermediates or roots you want to include in the PFX

Display certificates from a remote system (useful for trusting new certificates):

`openssl s_client -connect www.example.com:443 -servername www.example.com`

The `-servername` flag provides an SNI name to the s_client command. Usually this is the same as the hostname in the connect command, but a remote site can host different sites on the same IP/Port combo by relying on SNI name.

Generating Diffie-Hellman parameters (This command will take quite some time to complete):

`openssl dhparam -out dhparam.pem 2048`

Checking key, file, and CSR association:

Sometimes, you might lose track of which file was used for which operation. You can check the modulus of your files, and if they match, they are associated.

`openssl rsa -noout -modulus -in ./private.key`

`openssl req -noout -modulus -in ./myCSR.csr`

`openssl x509 -noout -modulus -in ./certificate.crt`

Commands can also be found here: https://link.keyko.com.au/opensslcommands

CHAPTER 8

HTTP/2 and HTTP/3

HTTP/2, defined in *RFC 7540*[1], is the latest official revision of the HTTP protocol specification. It provides full backwards compatibility for negotiating with browsers that only support lower protocol versions. HTTP/2 introduces some performance benefits over HTTP/1.1 its predecessor. HTTP/2 uses the HPACK algorithm to compress headers being sent across the wire. This lack of compression in the earlier version was identified as an area of opportunity, since values being sent are largely limited to the same few choices of values over and over again. HTTP/2 is a direct successor to Google's experiment with the SPDY protocol (Chapter 2: SPDY).

Despite HTTP/2's significant performance improvements, attributed to it running over TCP, if a segment needs to be retransmitted, everything comes screeching to a halt until it's been ACKed (TCP's shorthand for acknowledged). Google's QUIC protocol solves this problem by running over UDP, which is not inherently connection-oriented like TCP. Due to this, QUIC has to solve retransmission of dropped segments on its own. HTTP/3, in draft at the time of this writing, is based on QUIC (Chapter 2: QUIC) and also runs over UDP instead of TCP.

---

1. *https://www.rfc-editor.org/info/rfc7540*

HTTP/3 still does not benefit from widespread support. At the time of this writing, nginx for example does not support HTTP/3 (though through cloudflare's quiche[2] library HTTP/3 can be bolted on). As support becomes more mainstream, HTTP/3 will be put through its paces in the real world and we will see more and more companies make a push to adopt it. It is an exciting time to be a cryptography nerd!

Exciting new features

- HTTP/2's HPACK and HTTP/3's QPACK provide compression of commonly sent traffic.
- Not only does HTTP/3 mandate encryption, but the encrypted channel is established as part of establishing the connection itself.
- Multiple transfers can happen in parallel.

At the time of this writing, browsers are only beginning to introduce support for HTTP/3.

Browser	Version implemented	Date
Chrome	Stable build (79)	December 2019
Firefox	Stable build (72.0.1)	January 2020
Safari	Safari Technology Preview 104	April 2020
Edge	Edge (Canary build)	2020

Table 8.0: HTTP/3 Browser Support

---

2. *https://github.com/cloudflare/quiche*

The HTTPS Everywhere Movement

With the advent of HTTP/2, many argued that encryption should be required. Ultimately, it was decided that mandating this kind of change was outside the scope of a protocol revision, however major. In theory, HTTP/2 can be used without SSL/TLS. In practice, each and every major browser manufacturer only supports HTTP/2 over SSL/TLS. As a result, HTTP/3 requires encryption.

CHAPTER 9

Quick-Start Configuration

The following steps are enough to get you started using SSL/TLS on many popular web servers. Commands in this chapter which are geared towards Linux systems assume Ubuntu Linux, but the steps are very similar for Red Hat based distributions.

Apache

Apache is one of the most popular web servers on the planet, well-suited for serving dynamic content of many different types. Interestingly, Apache doesn't provide support for SSL/TLS out of the box, but rather via an extension called Mod_SSL. This guide assumes that you are logged into the web server as the root user.

First, let's install the base package.

```
apt-get install apache2
```

Now, we'll install support for SSL/TLS.

```
a2enmod ssl
```

The following will enable the default SSL/TLS configuration, serving the default content at */var/www/html*. It uses a self-signed SSL/TLS keypair to get you started, but we'll want to replace it with our own trusted keypair.

```
a2ensite ssl
```

We need to restart Apache for this configuration to take effect.

```
systemctl restart apache2
```

Before we provide Apache with our own configuration (more secure than the default), we need to do a couple of housekeeping tasks.

Allow TCP 443 through your host Firewall.

```
ufw allow 443
```

Create a directory to house our public and private keys.

```
mkdir /etc/apache2/ssl
```

Set the directory ownership to be that of the webserver user.

```
chown -R www-data:www-data /etc/apache2/ssl
```

Set the permissions on the directory so that only the webserver user (and of course, root) can access the key material (Chapter 6: File System ACLs).

```
chmod 700 /etc/apache2/ssl
```

Make this directory our current directory.

```
cd /etc/apache2/ssl
```

Generate a brand new private key. Keep this file private!

```
openssl genrsa -out ./myKey.key 2048
```

Using your private key, generate a certificate signing request which you will send off to your CA for the public certificate.

```
openssl req -new -key ./private.key -out ./mycsr.csr
```

As part of generating the CSR, you will be prompted for the following. These are discussed in Chapter 3: Certificate Signing Request.

```
Country Name (2 letter code) \[AU\]:
State or Province Name (full name) \[Some-State\]:
Locality Name (eg, city) \[\]:
Organization Name (eg, company) \[Internet Widgits Pty Ltd\]:
Organizational Unit Name (eg, section) \[\]:
Common Name (e.g. server FQDN or YOUR name) \[\]:
Email Address \[\]:
```

Generate Diffie-Hellman parameters (This command may take a long time to complete).

```
openssl dhparam -out ./dhparams.pem 2048
```

Now that we have everything we need, we can craft our configuration file. Before we do so, a brief lesson in enabling and disabling sites in Apache.

Apache has two directories for configuration files, **/etc/apache2/sites-available** and **/etc/apache2/sites-enabled**. The first directory houses configuration files that must have a .conf extension. The second directory contains only symlinks to the first directory, created with the following syntax:

```
ln -s /etc/apache2/sites-available/mySite.conf /etc/apache2/sites-enabled/mySite.conf
```

You can also use the command `a2ensite mySite.conf` to create the symlink.

Restart apache.

```
systemctl restart apache2
```

And your site will be available for use.

At this point, you either must get your certificate signed by a trusted party, or generate a self-signed certificate to use instead. The Certificate Authority will give you a copy of your certificate containing your public key, along with any intermediate certificates that must be included in your configuration. Root certificates do not need to be served by your webserver, as they must exist already in the end user's trust store.

Now, let's discuss Apache configuration files in depth. The following is an example configuration file, making use of the keys and parameters we created above. Save the following file (for example) as *secure.conf* inside **/etc/apache2/sites-available** and issue `a2ensite secure.conf` to make the configuration live.

```
<IfModule mod_ssl.c>
  <VirtualHost _default_:443>
    ServerAdmin webmaster@localhost
    DocumentRoot /var/www/html
    # Available loglevels: trace8, ..., trace1, debug, info, notice, warn,
    # error, crit, alert, emerg.
    # It is also possible to configure the loglevel for particular
    # modules, e.g.
    #LogLevel info ssl:warn
    ErrorLog ${APACHE_LOG_DIR}/error.log
    CustomLog ${APACHE_LOG_DIR}/access.log combined
    # For most configuration files from conf-available/, which are
    # enabled or disabled at a global level, it is possible to
    # include a line for only one particular virtual host. For example the
    # following line enables the CGI configuration for this host only
    # after it has been globally disabled with "a2disconf".
    #Include conf-available/serve-cgi-bin.conf
    # SSL Engine Switch:
    # Enable/Disable SSL for this virtual host.
    SSLEngine on

    # A self-signed (snakeoil) certificate can be created by installing
    # the ssl-cert package. See
    # /usr/share/doc/apache2/README.Debian.gz for more info.
    # If both key and certificate are stored in the same file, only the
    # SSLCertificateFile directive is needed.
    SSLCertificateFile /etc/apache2/ssl/mySignedCert.crt
    SSLCertificateKeyFile /etc/apache2/ssl/myKey.key

    # Server Certificate Chain:
    # Point SSLCertificateChainFile at a file containing the
    # concatenation of PEM encoded CA certificates which form the
    # certificate chain for the server certificate. Alternatively
    # the referenced file can be the same as SSLCertificateFile
    # when the CA certificates are directly appended to the server
    # certificate for convenience.
    SSLCertificateChainFile /etc/apache2/ssl/intermediates.crt
```

```
# Certificate Authority (CA):
# Set the CA certificate verification path where to find CA
# certificates for client authentication or alternatively one
# huge file containing all of them (file must be PEM encoded)
# Note: Inside SSLCACertificatePath you need hash symlinks
# to point to the certificate files. Use the provided
# Makefile to update the hash symlinks after changes.
#SSLCACertificatePath /etc/ssl/certs/
#SSLCACertificateFile /etc/apache2/ssl.crt/ca-bundle.crt

# Certificate Revocation Lists (CRL):
# Set the CA revocation path where to find CA CRLs for client
# authentication or alternatively one huge file containing all
# of them (file must be PEM encoded)
# Note: Inside SSLCARevocationPath you need hash symlinks
# to point to the certificate files. Use the provided
# Makefile to update the hash symlinks after changes.
#SSLCARevocationPath /etc/apache2/ssl.crl/
#SSLCARevocationFile /etc/apache2/ssl.crl/ca-bundle.crl

# Client Authentication (Type):
# Client certificate verification type and depth.  Types are
# none, optional, require and optional_no_ca.  Depth is a
# number which specifies how deeply to verify the certificate
# issuer chain before deciding the certificate is not valid.
#SSLVerifyClient require
#SSLVerifyDepth  10

# SSL Engine Options:
# Set various options for the SSL engine.
# FakeBasicAuth:
# Translate the client X.509 into a Basic Authorisation. This means that
# the standard Auth/DBMAuth methods can be used for access control. The
# user name is the `one line' version of the client's X.509 certificate.
# Note that no password is obtained from the user. Every entry in the
# user file needs this password: `xxj31ZMTZzkVA'.
# ExportCertData:
# This exports two additional environment variables: SSL_CLIENT_CERT and
# SSL_SERVER_CERT. These contain the PEM-encoded certificates of the
# server (always existing) and the client (only existing when client
# authentication is used). This can be used to import the certificates
# into CGI scripts.
# StdEnvVars:
```

```
# This exports the standard SSL/TLS related `SSL_*' environment
# variables. Per default this exportation is switched off for
# performance reasons, because the extraction step is an expensive
# operation and is usually useless for serving static content.
# So one usually enables the exportation for CGI and SSI requests only.
# OptRenegotiate:
# This enables optimized SSL connection renegotiation handling when SSL
# directives are used in per-directory context.
#SSLOptions +FakeBasicAuth +ExportCertData +StrictRequire

<FilesMatch "\.(cgi|shtml|phtml|php)$">
    SSLOptions +StdEnvVars
</FilesMatch>
<Directory /usr/lib/cgi-bin>
    SSLOptions +StdEnvVars
</Directory>

# SSL Protocol Adjustments:
# The safe and default but still SSL/TLS standard compliant shutdown
# approach is that mod_ssl sends the close notify alert but doesn't wait
# for the close notify alert from client. When you need a different
# shutdown approach you can use one of the following variables:
# ssl-unclean-shutdown:
# This forces an unclean shutdown when the connection is closed, i.e. no
# SSL close notify alert is send or allowed to received.  This violates
# the SSL/TLS standard but is needed for some brain-dead browsers. Use
# this when you receive I/O errors because of the standard approach where
# mod_ssl sends the close notify alert.
# ssl-accurate-shutdown:
# This forces an accurate shutdown when the connection is closed, i.e. a
# SSL close notify alert is send and mod_ssl waits for the close notify
# alert of the client. This is 100% SSL/TLS standard compliant, but in
# practice often causes hanging connections with brain-dead browsers. Use
# this only for browsers where you know that their SSL implementation
# works correctly.
# Notice: Most problems of broken clients are also related to the HTTP
# keep-alive facility, so you usually additionally want to disable
# keep-alive for those clients, too. Use variable "nokeepalive" for this.
# Similarly, one has to force some clients to use HTTP/1.0 to workaround
# their broken HTTP/1.1 implementation. Use variables "downgrade-1.0" and
# "force-response-1.0" for this.
# BrowserMatch "MSIE [2-6]" \
```

```
        # nokeepalive ssl-unclean-shutdown \
        # downgrade-1.0 force-response-1.0
        SSLProtocol -all +TLSv1.2
        SSLCipherSuite ECDHE-ECDSA-AES128-GCM-SHA256:ECDHE-RSA-AES128-GCM-SHA256:ECDHE-ECDSA-AES256-GCM-SHA384:ECDHE-RSA-AES256-GCM-SHA384:ECDHE-ECDSA-CHACHA20-POLY1305:ECDHE-RSA-CHACHA20-POLY1305:DHE-RSA-AES128-GCM-SHA256:DHE-RSA-AES256-GCM-SHA384

        SSLOpenSSLConfCmd DHParameters "/etc/apache2/ssl/dhparams.pem"
    </VirtualHost>
</IfModule>
```

Configuration file is also available via: https://link.keyko.com.au/apachesecure

NGINX

NGINX is right behind Apache in terms of popularity. Where Apache supports just about everything you can imagine via its module system, NGINX is much more judicious in the features it supports and the kinds of content it can serve. This results in a leaner codebase and that translates to faster performance.

First, install nginx:

```
apt-get install nginx
```

Change to the directory and create a home for our certificates and keys:

```
cd /etc/nginx
```

```
mkdir ssl
```

Set ownership:

```
chown -R www-data:www-data ssl
```

Set permissions:

```
chmod -R 700 ssl

cd ssl
```

Generate self-signed certificate (or, alternatively you can generate a CSR for a publicly signed certificate).

```
openssl req -x509 -nodes days 365 -newkey rsa:2048 -keyout ./certificate.key -out ./certificate.crt

openssl dhparam -out ./dhparam.pem 2048
```

Now, we edit the NGINX configuration file at **/etc/nginx/nginx.conf** to include some key settings for use with SSL/TLS. Specifically, we should change the ssl_protocols directive to include only TLS 1.2 and 1.3 and only use secure ciphers. Here is an example of a modified NGINX.conf:

```
user www-data;
worker_processes auto;
pid /run/nginx.pid;
include /etc/nginx/modules-enabled/*.conf;

events {
  worker_connections 768;
  # multi_accept on;
}

http {
    ##
    # Basic Settings
    ##
    sendfile on;
    tcp_nopush on;
    tcp_nodelay on;
    keepalive_timeout 65;
    types_hash_max_size 2048;
    # server_tokens off;
    # server_names_hash_bucket_size 64;
    # server_name_in_redirect off;
    include /etc/nginx/mime.types;
    default_type application/octet-stream;
```

```
      ##
      # SSL Settings
      ##
      ssl_protocols TLSv1.2 TLSv1.3; # Dropping SSLv3, ref: POODLE
      ssl_prefer_server_ciphers on;

      ##
      # Logging Settings
      ##
      access_log /var/log/nginx/access.log;
      error_log /var/log/nginx/error.log;

      ##
      # Gzip Settings
      ##
      gzip on;
      # gzip_vary on;
      # gzip_proxied any;
      # gzip_comp_level 6;
      # gzip_buffers 16 8k;
      # gzip_http_version 1.1;
      # gzip_types text/plain text/css application/json application/javascript text/xml application/xml application/xm+rss;text/javascript;

      ##
      # Virtual Host Configs
      ##
      include /etc/nginx/conf.d/*.conf;
      include /etc/nginx/sites-enabled/*;
}
```

Configuration file is also available via: https://link.keyko.com.au/nginxsecure

Next, we must provide a site configuration. NGINX is capable of serving multiple sites either by having the sites listening on different ports or by using SNI (Chapter 2: SNI).

Create a file at **/etc/nginx/sites-available/examplesite** And populate it with the following:

```
# Specify the TLS versions
#ssl_protocols TLSv1.2;
#ssl_prefer_server_ciphers on;


# Mozilla Ciphersuites Recommendation
# Use this for all devices supports
#ssl_ciphers 'ECDHE-ECDSA-AES256-GCM-SHA384:ECDHE-RSA-AES256-GCM-SHA384:ECDHE-ECDSA-CHACHA20-POLY1305:ECDHE-RSA-CHACHA20-POLY1305:ECDHE-ECDSA-AES128-GCM-SHA256:ECDHE-RSA-AES128-GCM-SHA256:ECDHE-ECDSA-AES256-SHA384:ECDHE-RSA-AES256-SHA384:ECDHE-ECDSA-AES128-SHA256:ECDHE-RSA-AES128-SHA256';

# Use the DHPARAM key and ECDH curve >= 256bit
ssl_ecdh_curve secp384r1;
ssl_dhparam /etc/nginx/ssl/dhparam.pem;

server_tokens off;
ssl_session_timeout 1d;
ssl_session_cache shared:SSL:50m;
ssl_session_tickets off;

# Enable HTTP Strict-Transport-Security
add_header Strict-Transport-Security "max-age=63072000; preload";

# Enable OSCP Stapling for Nginx web server
# If you're using the SSL from Letsencrypt,
# use the 'chain.pem' certificate
ssl_stapling on;
ssl_stapling_verify on;

# XSS Protection for Nginx web server
add_header X-Frame-Options DENY;
add_header X-XSS-Protection "1; mode=block";
add_header X-Content-Type-Options nosniff;
add_header X-Robots-Tag none;

server {
    listen 80;
    listen [::]:80;
    server_name example.schattenconsulting.com;
    return 301 https://$host$request_uri;
}
```

```
server {
    listen 443 ssl http2;
    listen [::]:443 ssl http2;

    root     /var/www/html;
    index index.html;
    server_name  domain.com; ### Enter your domain here
    error_log /var/log/nginx/error.log warn;

    # SSL Configuration
    ssl_certificate /etc/nginx/ssl/certificate.crt; ### Path to your Certificate
    ssl_certificate_key /etc/nginx/ssl/certificate.key; ### Path to your Private Key

    location ~ /.well-known {
            allow all;
    }

    location / {
            try_files $uri $uri/ =404;
    }

    location = /favicon.ico {
            log_not_found off;
            access_log off;
    }

    location = /robots.txt {
            allow all;
            log_not_found off;
            access_log off;
    }

    location ~* \.(js|css|png|jpg|jpeg|gif|ico)$ {
            expires max;
            log_not_found off;
    }
}
```

Finally, we create a symlink to make the site active.

```
ln -s /etc/nginx/sites-available/examplesite /etc/nginx/sites-enabled
service nginx restart
```

Configuration file is also available via: htttps://link.keyko.com.au/nginxsite

Microsoft Windows and IIS

This guide assumes you're running a fully up to date instance of Windows Server 2019 with the IIS role installed.

First, we want to generate a certificate keypair to be used by the webserver for encryption. At the top level, the "Server Certificates" module allows you to work with SSL/TLS certificates. There are more advanced options in the Certificates MMC snap-in, but that is beyond the scope of this guide.

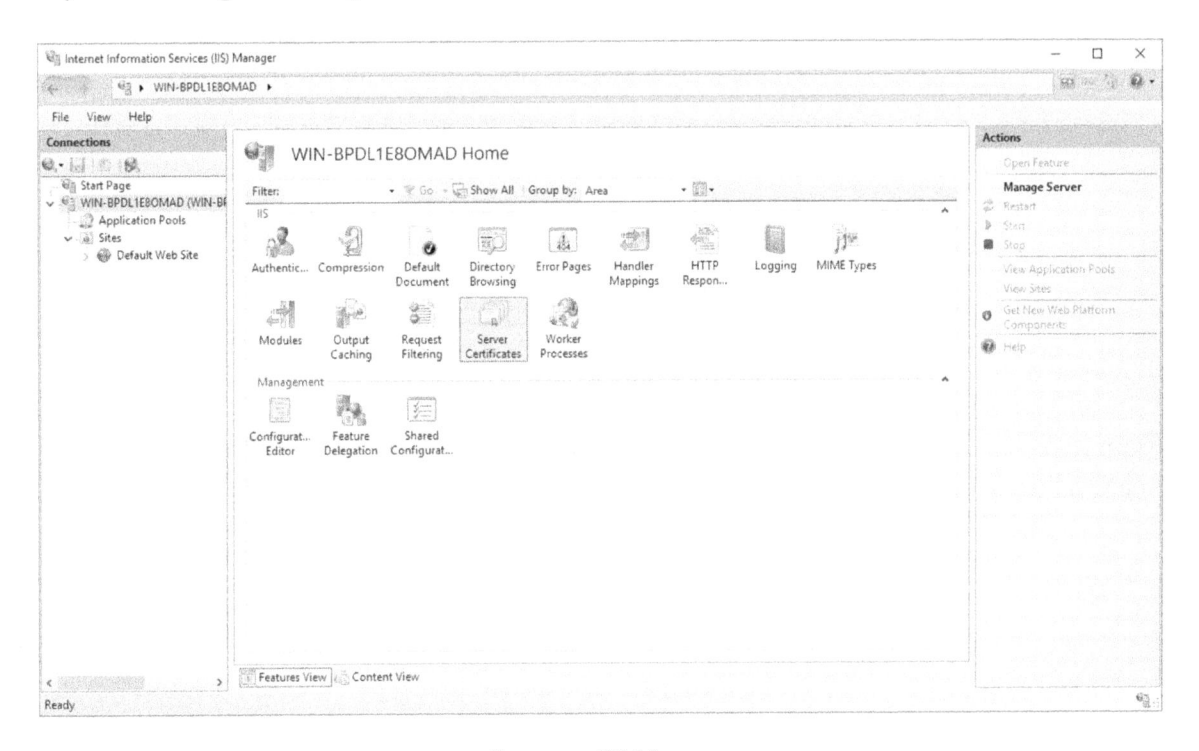

Image 9.0: IIS Manager

If we navigate into **Server Certificates** we can see our options in the right pane.

Image 9.1: IIS Manager, Server Certificates

From here, we can either generate a self signed certificate, or create a CSR to be submitted to a Certificate Authority for digital signature.

Whatever method you choose, once you have a certificate available, right click on an available site and select **Edit Bindings**.

Image 9.2: IIS Manager, Edit Bindings

From here, we can add a new port binding and select from the available certificates if the binding type is HTTPS.

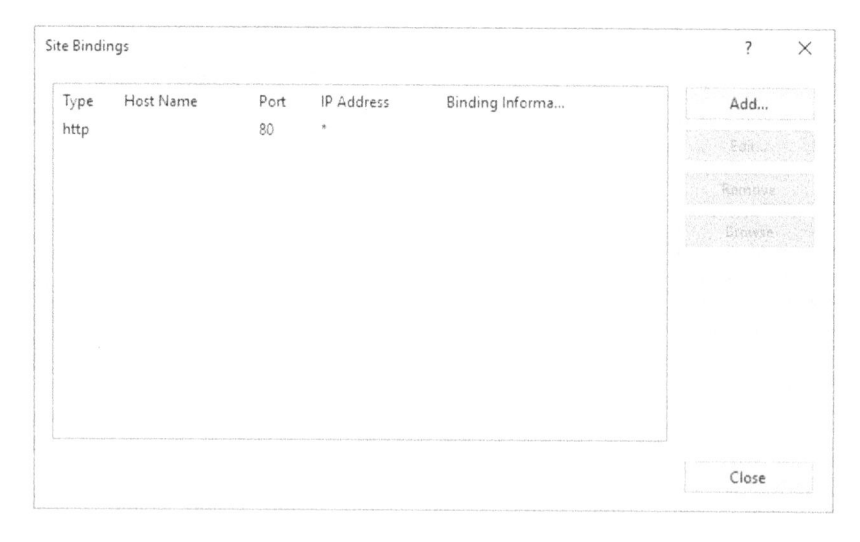

Image 9.3: IIS Manager, Site Bindings

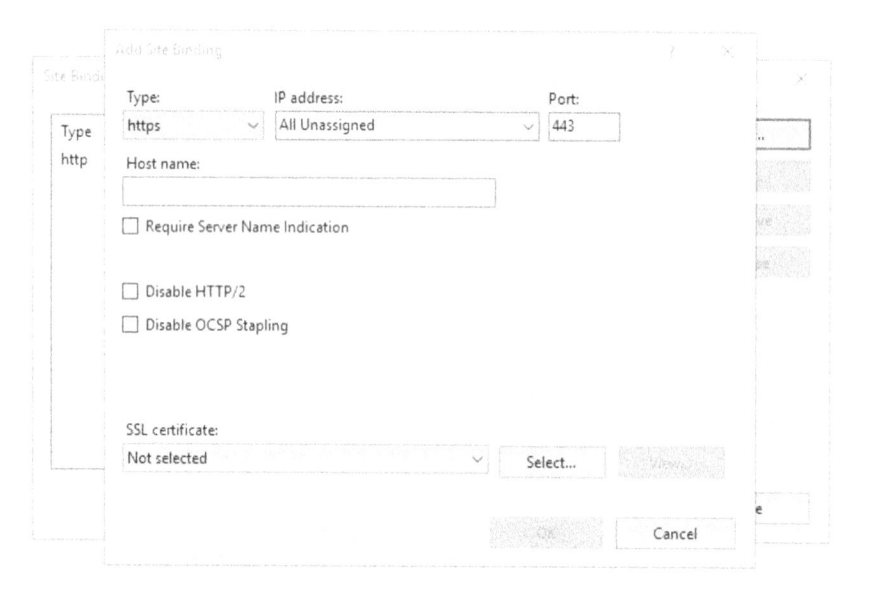

Image 9.4: IIS Manager, Add Site Binding

100 • Microsoft Windows and IIS

SCHANNEL Registry changes

Out of the box, even Server 2019 still supports TLS 1.0 and TLS 1.1 but they should be disabled for security reasons. At the time of this writing, Server 2019 does not yet support TLS 1.3.

In order to make these changes, we must create registry keys that SCHANNEL (the part of the Windows Operating System that handles SSL/TLS) will respect. This can be done either through Regedit, or via Windows Powershell.

For reference, the following powershell will disable TLS 1.0 and 1.1. After making these changes, restart the machine for it to take effect.

```powershell
New-Item 'HKLM:\SYSTEM\CurrentControlSet\Control\SecurityProviders\SCHANNEL\Protocols\TLS 1.0\Server' -Force | Out-Null
New-ItemProperty -path 'HKLM:\SYSTEM\CurrentControlSet\Control\SecurityProviders\SCHANNEL\Protocols\TLS 1.0\Server' -name 'Enabled' -value '0' -PropertyType 'DWord' -Force | Out-Null
New-ItemProperty -path 'HKLM:\SYSTEM\CurrentControlSet\Control\SecurityProviders\SCHANNEL\Protocols\TLS 1.0\Server' -name 'DisabledByDefault' -value 1 -PropertyType 'DWord' -Force | Out-Null
New-Item 'HKLM:\SYSTEM\CurrentControlSet\Control\SecurityProviders\SCHANNEL\Protocols\TLS 1.0\Client' -Force | Out-Null
New-ItemProperty -path 'HKLM:\SYSTEM\CurrentControlSet\Control\SecurityProviders\SCHANNEL\Protocols\TLS 1.0\Client' -name 'Enabled' -value '0' -PropertyType 'DWord' -Force | Out-Null
New-ItemProperty -path 'HKLM:\SYSTEM\CurrentControlSet\Control\SecurityProviders\SCHANNEL\Protocols\TLS 1.0\Client' -name 'DisabledByDefault' -value 1 -PropertyType 'DWord' -Force | Out-Null
New-Item 'HKLM:\SYSTEM\CurrentControlSet\Control\SecurityProviders\SCHANNEL\Protocols\TLS 1.1\Server' -Force | Out-Null
New-ItemProperty -path 'HKLM:\SYSTEM\CurrentControlSet\Control\SecurityProviders\SCHANNEL\Protocols\TLS 1.1\Server' -name 'Enabled' -value '0' -PropertyType 'DWord' -Force | Out-Null
New-ItemProperty -path 'HKLM:\SYSTEM\CurrentControlSet\Control\SecurityProviders\SCHANNEL\Protocols\TLS 1.1\Server' -name 'DisabledByDefault' -value 1 -PropertyType 'DWord' -Force | Out-Null
New-Item 'HKLM:\SYSTEM\CurrentControlSet\Control\SecurityProviders\SCHANNEL\Protocols\TLS 1.1\Client' -Force | Out-Null
New-ItemProperty -path 'HKLM:\SYSTEM\CurrentControlSet\Control\SecurityProviders\SCHANNEL\Protocols\TLS 1.1\Client' -name 'Enabled' -value '0' -PropertyType 'DWord' -Force | Out-Null
New-ItemProperty -path 'HKLM:\SYSTEM\CurrentControlSet\Control\SecurityProviders\SCHANNEL\Protocols\TLS 1.1\Client' -name 'DisabledByDefault' -value 1 -PropertyType 'DWord' -Force | Out-Null
```

You can find these Powershell commands here: https://link.keyko.com.au/schanneldisabletls

Java and Tomcat

Install Tomcat.

`apt-get update`

`apt-get install tomcat8`

Generating a java keystore.

`cd /etc/tomcat8`

`/usr/bin/keytool -genkey -alias tomcat -keyalg RSA -keystore /etc/tomcat8/keystore.jks`

This will prompt for a keystore password. Use the default keystore password of *"changeit"*.

You will be prompted for information to complete the keystore creation.

Once the java keystore has been created, we need to configure Tomcat to use it for SSL/TLS connections to our server.

`vim /etc/tomcat/8/server.xml`

Make sure to include a connector that looks like the following:

```
<Connector port="8443" protocol="org.apache.coyote.http11.Http11NioProtocol" maxThreads="150" SSLEnabled="true" >
    <SSLHostConfig protocols="TLSv1.2,TLSv1.3">
        <Certificate certificateKeystoreFile="conf/keystore.jks" type="RSA" />
    </SSLHostConfig>
</Connector>
```

Configuration file is also available via: https://link.keyko.com.au/tomcatconnector

Note that we only want to allow secure TLS connections over TLSv1.2 or 1.3.

Restart Tomcat.

```
service tomcat8 restart
```

Allow connection through our Firewall.

```
ufw allow 8443
```

cPanel

CPanel is an extremely popular multi-tenanted web-based management software commonly used by Virtual Private Server (VPS) resellers. For example, if you're ever working with HostGator, they're giving you access to your tenant via CPanel.

The CPanel interface commonly looks like this (image 9.5):

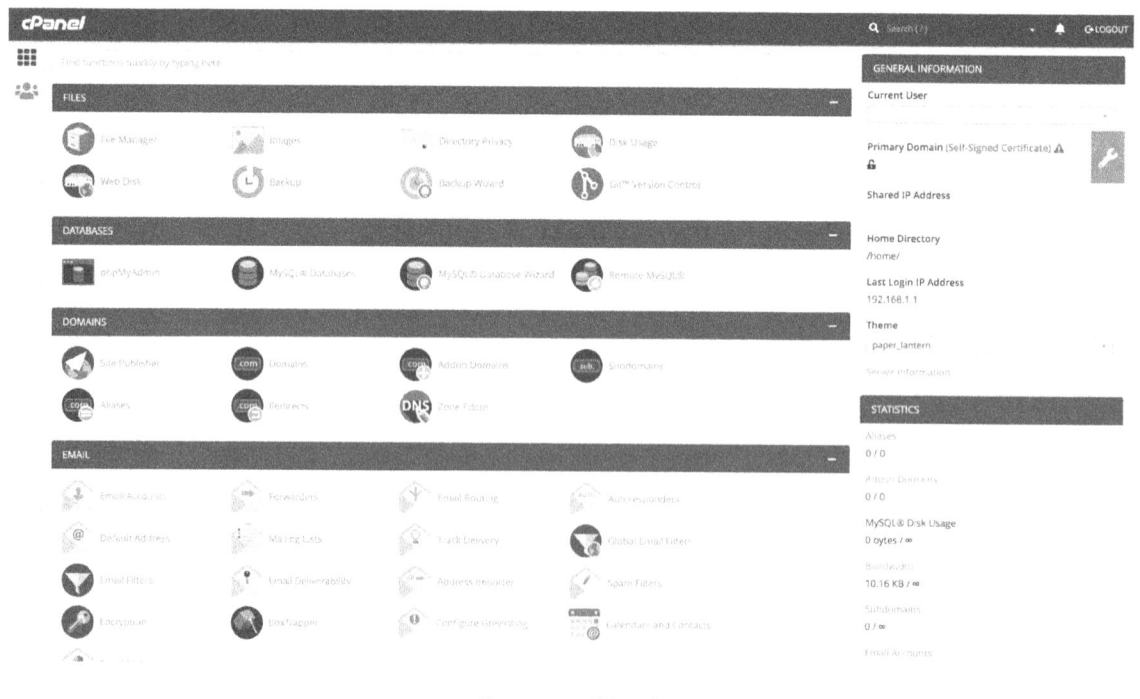

Image 9.5: CPanel

...And consists of various modules. It is geared towards power-users rather than professional Systems Administrators. While powerful, certain aspects of CPanel can be frustrating since access to backend services are brokered by the web-based GUI.

Luckily, adding an SSL/TLS certificate is not one of those common frustrations. The process is pretty seamless. Navigate to the SSL/TLS module (under the Security Heading).

Image 9.6: CPanel, Security Tab

You will be greeted with the following (image 9.7):

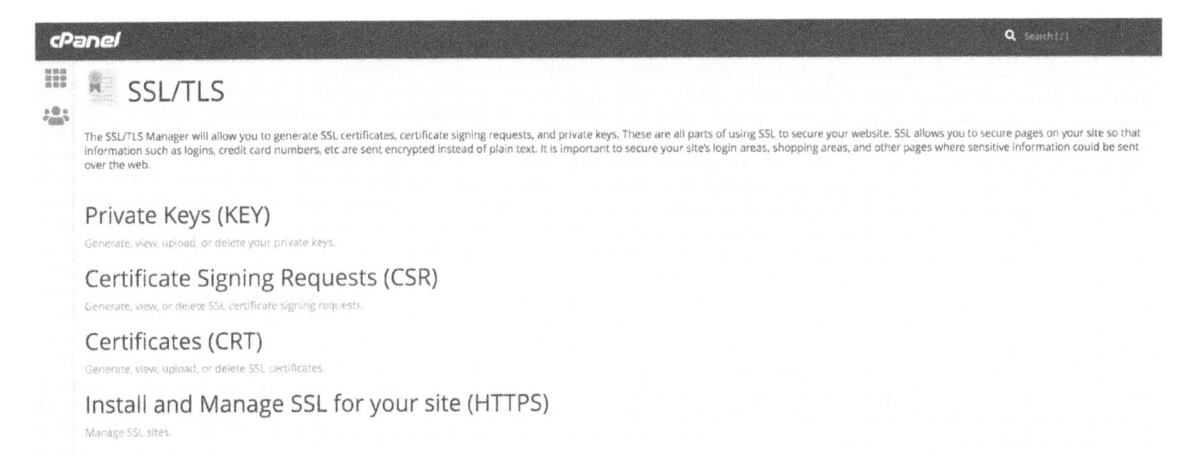

Image 9.7: CPanel, SSL/TLS Module

Select **Install and Manage SSL for your site**.

You are expected to already have a signed certificate from a trusted CA in Base64 format as well as its private key (also in Base64).

First you will select your domain (any domain you're allowed to manage within CPanel will appear here).

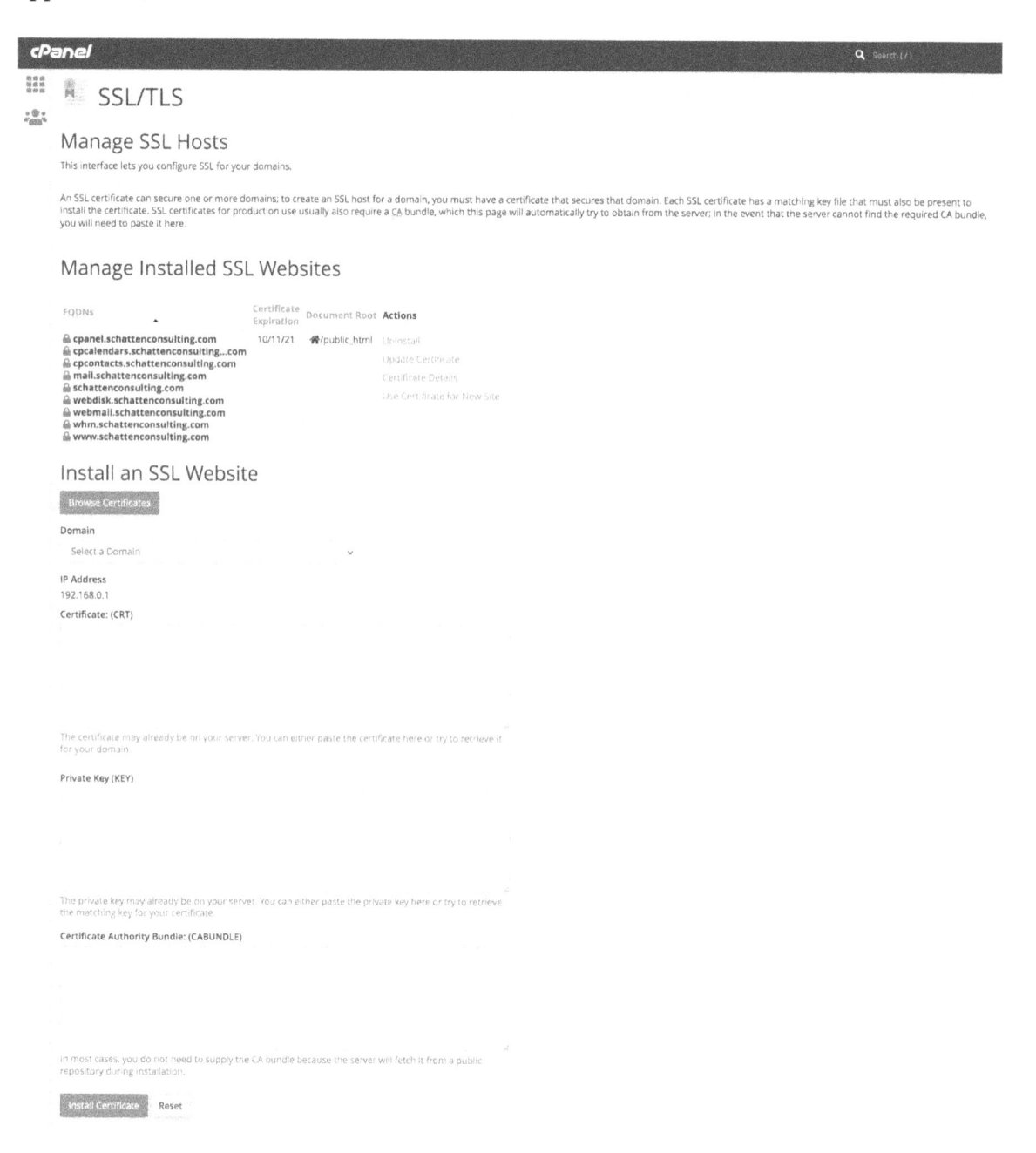

Image 9.8: CPanel, Install an SSL Website

You will paste in your certificate and private key.

Under **Certificate Authority Bundle,** provide any intermediate certificates required for the end user to chain back to the established root certificate present in their certificate store.

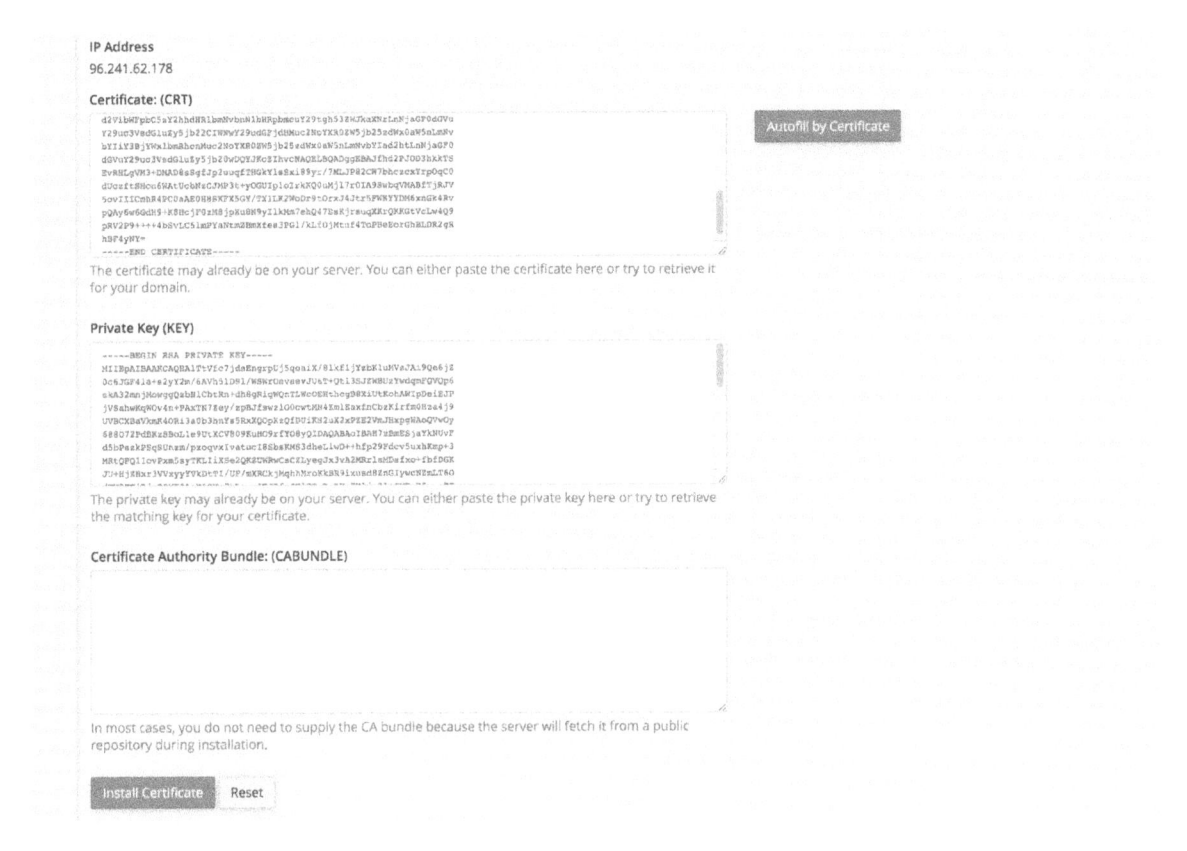

Image 9.9: CPanel, Install SSL Filled

Select **Install Certificate** at the bottom of the page (image 9.9). The certificate will immediately be used to answer requests to the domain defined.

Chapter 9: Quick-Start Configuration • 107

CONCLUSION

We live in exciting times. The next decade will bring changes to the landscape of digital cryptography that we can now barely fathom. Governments worldwide vie to close the Pandora's Box that is digital encryption, using the relative inaccessibility of knowledge on cryptosystems to garner support for things such as government sponsored back doors and elaborate key escrow systems.

While the legitimacy of whether this furthers protecting its citizenry is still up for debate, there is no question that such actions tilt the balance of power.

Meanwhile, quantum computing pushes the boundaries of what we once thought possible. By 2023, IBM anticipates the first 1000 qubit quantum computer. This challenges many encryption schemes which rely upon the fact that our one-way functions are easy to compute and difficult to reverse. The ciphers we will be using to secure digital communications in the year 2030 do not yet exist. It is in this spirit that we amend our most fundamental of assertions: SSL/TLS must be accessible to everyone because it is foundational to our modern ~~online~~ world.

TERMINOLOGY

128-Bit or 256-Bit encryption

This is the size of the symmetric key used to encrypt data with AES (such as between a web browser and web server). The larger the number, the harder it is to brute force, however, for all practical purposes, neither 128-Bit nor 256-Bit keys can be cracked by any computers that exist today.

Asymmetric Encryption

This is a form of encryption using two different but linked keys. One is used to encrypt while the other is used to decrypt. Asymmetric Encryption is also referred to as "Public Key Cryptography".

Authentication

The process of verifying that a user is who they claim to be. In asymmetric cryptography, authentication is reliant on the fact that a private key is known only to its owner. We take advantage of this 1:1 relationship to allow proof of ownership.

Authenticity

Using a series of predefined checks to ensure the object is not a forgery.

Authorization

Authorization defines the permission a user has to a resource.

Block Ciphers

Data is split into fixed-length blocks (e.g. 64-bit or 128-bit blocks,) and then encrypted.

Brute-Force Attack

An attack against a system which operates by trying every possible combination.

CA/Browser Forum

Governing entity responsible for establishing the standards of digital certificates and Certificate Authorities.

Decrypting

The process of taking ciphertext and reversing it back into plaintext.

Certificate

A container around a keypair which often also confirms the identity of an organisation or user and is used to verify data being exchanged over a network. It can contain additional useful attributes, such as CA signature, expiration dates and revocation information.

Certificate expiry

The date a Certificate expires and after which it can no longer be used or trusted (except in the case of a time-stamped Code-Signing Certificate).

Certificate Revocation

Revocation is the process by which a certificate can be retroactively invalided by its signer. Typically, this is published as a CRL or handled via OCSP.

Certificate Revocation List (CRL)

A list of Certificates issued by the Certificate Authority that are no longer valid and trusted. This list is made public so browsers can query it and check the authenticity of a Certificate by using its thumbprint as a selector.

Certification Authority (CA)

An organisation that is responsible for the creation, issuance, revocation, and management of Certificates.

Certificate Signing Request (CSR)

A request containing the information required for a CA to issue a signed public key.

Chain of Trust

Determines how a Certificate is linked back to a trusted Certificate Authority. Root certificates must pre-exist in the client's trusted root store. Node certificates and intermediate certificates must "chain" back to a trusted root certificate.

Checksum

A checksum is a small-sized datum derived from a block of digital data for the purpose of verifying data integrity.

Ciphers

Ciphers are algorithms used to encrypt and decrypt data.

Digital Signature

An electronic rather than written signature. It can be attached to a message, whether it is encrypted or not, so that the receiver can be sure of the sender's identity and that the message has arrived intact.

Digital Signature Algorithm (DSA)

An algorithm for producing digital signatures.

Domain Name System (DNS)

An Internet service that translates domain names into IP addresses. When you type a domain name into a browser, it queries a DNS Server and directs your browser to connect to the correct server which hosts the wanted website.

Domain Validation (DV)

The validation of ownership in relation to a specific domain name.

Elliptical Curve Cryptography (ECC)

A public key encryption algorithm based on elliptic curve theory. It can be used to create faster, smaller, and more efficient cryptographic keys.

Encryption

The process of hiding a message (plaintext) by transforming it into ciphertext.

End-Entity Certificate

A digitally-signed statement issued by a Certificate Authority to an organization or individual.

Extended Validation (EV)

The validation of the requesting organisation that has a more in-depth process of approval than standard organisation validation.

FQDN

A fully qualified domain name, sometimes also referred to as an absolute domain name.

HTTP (Hypertext Transfer Protocol)

HTTP is an application layer (layer 7) protocol used to transmit data containing text, images, and links over a network. On its own, HTTP is not encrypted.

HTTPS (Hypertext Transfer Protocol Secure)

HTTPS refers to tunneling the HTTP protocol over SSL/TLS.

Key Pair

A "key pair" refers to two mathematically linked asymmetric keys. Through the use of one-way functions, it is easy to generate the keypair, but impossible to derive one from the other after the fact. Information encrypted with the public key can only be decrypted by the private key (and vice versa).

Key Size

The number of bits in a key used by a cryptographic algorithm. More bits mean stronger security.

Individual Validation (IV)

The process in which a Certificate Authority has validated the identity of the individual applicant: Usually an individual person and not an organisation.

Intermediate Certificate

A Certificate that is signed by either a Root Certificate or another Intermediate Certificate, and then signs End-Entity Certificates.

Malware

A malicious program designed by hackers to steal information or damage systems.

MD5

An old hashing method that creates a 128-bit hash value. MD5 should not be used for cryptographic purposes.

MITM (Man-in-the-middle)

An attacker covertly listens on the wire between two communicating parties.

Multi-Domain Certificate

A Certificate that has the ability to secure more than one domain name. The list of domains that can be secured will be contained within the certificate.

Online Certificate Status Protocol (OCSP)

An Internet protocol used for obtaining the revocation status of an X.509 certificate.

Organisation Validation (OV)

When the company is validated, rather than just the domain. The Certificate Authority runs checks on the company to ensure they are a legal operating company.

Padding

When a specified fixed-length is required and that length is not met, padding (usually random data or 0's) is used to bring it to the required length.

Protocol

An agreed upon method for sending and receiving information.

Private Key

One part of a Key Pair (Private and Public Keys) in asymmetric encryption. It can encrypt or decrypt data for a single transaction but cannot do both. It should never be shared.

Public Key

One part of a Key Pair (Private and Public Keys) in asymmetric encryption that is shared with anyone. It can encrypt or decrypt data for a single transaction but cannot do both.

Root Certificate

A self-signed certificate from a top level Certificate Authority to identify itself and to facilitate verification of issued Certificates. Pre-defined Root certificates are distributed with web browsers and operating systems.

RSA

A cryptographic algorithm used both to generate asymmetric keys and generate / validate digital signatures.

Self-signed Certificate

A Certificate signed with the owner's own private key and not a 3rd party Certificate Authority.

SHA-1

An older cryptographic hash function that produces 160-bit hash value.

SHA-2

A modern cryptographic algorithm that has replaced the earlier SHA-1 algorithm.

SNI (Server Name Indication)

A TLS protocol extension. SNI allows a server to present multiple certificates on the same IP address and TCP port number. The SNI name is sent unencrypted before SSL/TLS begins.

Secure Sockets Layer (SSL)

A security protocol to secure communication between the sender and receiver.

SSL/TLS Key

Another common name for the Private Key

SSL/TLS keystore

A repository of security certificates – either client certificates or public key certificates and their corresponding private keys.

SSL/TLS handshake

The start of an SSL session that includes steps such as – client hello, server hello, authentication and pre-master secret, decryption and master secret, and session key generation.

SSL/TLS Port / HTTPS Port

The port allotted to the web server for SSL traffic. Generally, SSL sessions are made on Port 443.

SSL/TLS Proxy

A proxy sits in the middle of two communicating parties. A bad actor could set up a proxy for the purposes of a MITM attack, or a legitimate administrator could set up a proxy for the purposes of network administration. An SSL/TLS proxy can be either terminating or non-terminating, depending on whether traffic is decrypted and encrypted, or simply passed along unaltered. An SSL/TLS proxy is also useful for putting in front of a resource which is unable to handle encryption on its own.

Symmetric Encryption

Uses the same key to encrypt and decrypt secure messages.

Transport Layer Security (TLS)

A cryptographic protocol that provides secure data communications. The TLS protocol aims primarily to provide privacy and data integrity between two or more communicating computer applications.

Thumbprint

The hash of a certificate which serves as a unique identifier.

Unified Communication Certificate (UCC Certificate)

A digital security certificate which allows multiple hostnames to be secured by a single certificate.

Wildcard Certificate

Secures unlimited subdomains with a single asterisk in the Certificate Common Name: *.domain.com

X.509

A standard defining the format of public key certificates.

INDEX

A

Access Control Lists, 74-75
    ACLs
Advanced Encryption Standard, 19-20
    AES
    Output Feedback, OFB
    Counter Mode, CTR
Algorithm, 3
Apache, 85-91
ASN, 70
Asymmetric Cryptography, 7-8
    Asymmetric Encryption
Authentication, 25-27

B

Base64, 70, 79
Binary, 70, 79
Bit, 5-6, 16, 59
Block Ciphers, 13
BREACH, 66
Buffer Overread Attack, 65

C

Caesar Cipher, 3
Certificate Authorities, 44-46, 49
    CA
    Root Certificate Authorities, 44-45
    Intermediate Certificate Authority, 45
    Internal Certificate Authorities, 46
Certificate Authority Authorisation, 47-49
    CAA
    CAA Record, 48
Certificate Cross Certification, 46
Certificate Extensions, 54
Certificate Fields, 52
Certificate Lifecycle, 42-44
    Key Pair Generation, 42-43
    Validation, 43
    Issuance, 43
    Revocation, 43
Certificate Revocation List, 47
    CRL
Certificate Signing Request, 42
    CSR
Certificate Transparency, 30-31
    Certificate Logs

Monitors
Auditors
Cipher Strength, 16
Cipher Suite, 29-30
Ciphertext, 5
Client Certificates, 57
Client Hello, 8, 24
Code Signing Certificates, 57
Collision Attack, 63
Common Name, 42
CPanel, 104-107
CRIME, 66
CryptoAPI, 72
Cryptography, 3

D

Data Encryption Standard, 17
   DES
   Electronic Code Book, ECB
   Chain Block Coding, CBC
Cipher Feedback, CFB
Datagram Transport Layer Security, 36
   UDP
   DTLS
Decryption, 5
Diffie-Hellman, 33
Digest, 11
Digital Signatures, 12, 63
Domain Validation, 43
   DV
DROWN, 66

E

Elliptic Curve Cryptography, 17
   ECC
Encryption, 3
   HTTPS Encryption, 28
Exchange Server, 56
Explicit SSL/TLS, 34

F

File Formats, 70-73
   PEM
   CRT
   PFX
   CER
   PKCS
File Transfer Protocol, 34-35
   FTPS
Forward Secrecy, 33

H

Hardware Security Module, 73
   HSM
HTTPS, 21, 81-83
   Handshake Protocol, 22-23
HTTP Public Key Pinning, 33
   HPKP
HTTP Strict Transport Security, 32
   HSTS
HTTPS Stripping, 32
Hashing, 11
   Hash

Hash Function
Heartbleed, 65

I

IIS, 97-100
Initialization Vector, 13
Insecure Renegotiation, 29
Issuance, 43

J

Java, 72, 103-104

K

Key, 15, 71-73
   Public Key
   Private Key
Key Escrow, 62
Key Exchange, 24
Key Size, 16, 59-60
Key Space, 59
Keystore, 72

L

Linux, 72
   Unix
Lightweight Directory Access Protocol, 35
   LDAPS
   OpenLDAP

Active Directory

M

Macintosh, 78
   Mac
Man-In-The-Middle Attack, 60-61, 63
   MITM
Master Secret, 9

N

Nationstate, 67
.NET, 72
NGINX, 91-96

O

Online Certificate Status Protocol, 47
   OCSP
OpenSSL, 77-80

P

Padding Attack, 65
PEM, 70
Perfect Forward Secrecy, 33
   PFS
PFX, 70
PKCS, 73
Plaintext, 5
POODLE, 65

Protocols, 8, 21
Proxy, 63
   Middlebox
Public Key Infrastructure, 39-41
   PKI

Q

Quantum Computing, 67
QUIC, 37-38

R

Renegotiation, 29
Revocation, 43, 47
Root Store, 39
RSA, 17

S

Schannel, 72, 101-102
SCTP, 37
Server Hello, 9, 24-25
Server Name Indication, 31-32
   SNI
Session, 9, 22
Session ID, 24
Session Keys, 9, 24
Shared Secret, 6
SHA, 14, 46
Signature Algorithms, 25
Signatures, 12
Signature Forgery, 63

Simple Mail Transfer Protocol, 33-34
   SMTPS
SPDY, 37
Secure Socket Layer, 8-9, 12
   SSL
SSL Striping, 64
StartTLS, 34
Stream Ciphers, 13
Strict Transport Security, 32
Subject Alternative Name, 55-56
   SAN
   SAN Certificates, 56
Symmetric Cryptography, 5-6
   Symmetric Encryption

T

TLS, 8-9, 12-15
Tomcat, 103-104
Transmission Control Protocol, 36
   TCP

U

Unified Communications Certificates, 56
   UCC
Upstream Compromise, 61

V

Validation, 43
Vulnerabilities, 59

W

Wildcard Certificates, 55
Windows, 72, 78, 97-100

X

X.509, 51
    X.509 Certificate